A Spiritual Odyssey

Timely Visits to Biblical Times

ALBERT DOUGLAS

All Scripture quotations, unless otherwise indicated, are from The King James Version. The KJV is public domain in the United States.

ISBN: 978-1-945975-98-1

Published by EA Books Publishing a division of Living Parables of Central Florida, Inc. a 501c3
EABooksPublishing.com

A Spiritual Odyssey

"A Spiritual Odyssey" is truly inspiring. This book, better than any other that I have read, really shows us how we can practically travel back in time with the use of our imagination and make the biblical history of redemption come alive in our daily lives.

Dr. Norman Wise
Doctor of Theology
Executive Director of Living Water Counseling
Co-author of the book with Dr. James Kennedy,
Your Prodigal Child

Remember a time long ago. Think about all the past generations. Ask your fathers to remind you, and your leaders to tell you.

Deuteronomy 32:7

This book is dedicated to all believers who seek to have the mind of Christ, and yearn to have the heart of God.

CONTENTS

Introduction

No doubt as a believer you have been fascinated with the biblical accounts of holy men of God who had personal encounters with the divine creator. What if you were there? What if you could travel back through time to the past to witness such encounters? What if you could witness Abraham speaking face to face with God in the flesh, and then see him offering up his son, Isaac, as a sacrifice to God? And what if you could witness Moses at the burning bush, and could be there with Elijah as he confronted the wind, the earthquake, and the fire? Such an experience would be indeed unforgettable. But what would be even more unforgettable by far, would be to witness Jesus in the manger, Jesus on the Mount of Transfiguration, Jesus on the cross, and the resurrected Jesus leaving his tomb. What an awesome and glorious experience that would be!

Unfortunately, you cannot physically travel back through time to the past in order to witness the momentous events of the Bible. But mentally speaking, it is a completely different matter. God has given us a special gift, the gift of memory (remembrance of God's Word) to take us back to past events. And with this special gift of memory he has also given us the unique gift of imagination to relive the past. There is no time barrier to our thoughts, so our thoughts can soar on the wings of memory and imagination to the distant past. Indeed, with the God-given gifts of memory and imagination, the mind can become a kind of mental time machine to take us on a spiritual odyssey back through time.

Going on a journey to biblical times would be an act of obedience to God in light of the teaching of the Bible requiring believers to mentally revisit the past. According to the Bible, every believer should mentally revisit the momentous events of biblical times. Jesus says, "For as often as you eat this bread and drink this cup, you show the Lord's death till He comes. Do this in remembrance of me," (1 Corinthians 11:26). Also, in the Old Testament, we are commanded to do the following: "Remember a time long ago. Think about all the past generations. Ask your fathers to remind you, and your leaders to tell you." (Deuteronomy 32:7)

Therefore, in view of the teaching of the Bible about remembering the past, it seems evident that God requires all people of faith to be mental time travelers of the Bible. We should always endeavor to travel back in time through the remembrance of his Word, and the guidance of the Holy Spirit, in order to revisit and relive the past. Why does the Lord require us to constantly remember the recorded history of biblical events? I believe the answer can be found in the need to nurture our faith so that we will always be spiritually connected to God. Consequently, we should make timely visits to spend time with the Lord, by traveling mentally to the momentous events of the Bible, in order to strengthen our faith in God and enhance our loving bond with Christ Jesus as Savior and Lord.

On your spiritual odyssey, when you use your mind to transport yourself – your innermost being– to the events of redemption, you will also experience a wonderful spiritual blessing as you obey the Lord's injunction in remembering, or mentally visiting the past. Indeed, there is no greater blessing than to enter the presence of God, when in obedience to the Lord's injunction, you allow the mind to take you back to the past, to the time of your redemption– to His birth, transfiguration, crucifixion and resurrection. The Bible says, "Blessed is the man who meditates upon the word day and night." (Psalm 1) In his holy presence you experience the wonderful blessings of perfect peace, unspeakable joy, renewed strength, and the power for living.

Before embarking on your timely visits to certain events in the Bible, it is necessary to spiritually prepare your hearts and minds. You should always prepare yourself by reading the Bible and prayerfully meditating upon the scriptural account of the events to be visited. The Word of God then becomes a lamp and a light for your journey. Indeed, throughout this book, you will be encouraged to endeavor to bridle and restrain your imagination from wandering beyond the revealed truth of the Bible. You should always be mindful that a vain or carnal imagination can cause a shipwreck to your spiritual journey.

As you mentally visit biblical events you will be there with great men of God to share their awesome encounter with God. Through the God given gift of your imagination you will feel what they are feeling, and experience the wonder of their divine encounter. You will be a silent observer and interpreter of their words and actions, as they face their moment of truth before God. Indeed, as you share in their encounters with God, the loving kindness and the tender mercy of almighty God will be revealed in the most wonderful way.

It has been said that experience is the best teacher. For example, if you experience a certain event, rather than just hearing about it, then such event becomes more meaningful and more life changing. Through the gift of memory (remembrance of God's Word) and the gift of imagination, which allows you to transport yourself mentally through time, you will experience in a personal way these events of the Bible. As a result such events will become more meaningful. Therefore, you will no doubt gain new spiritual insights and learn important lessons from God's Word as you mentally visit biblical events.

Furthermore, the remembrance of God's Word connects you to the spiritual realities of the past. The gift of memory pertains to past events– what God has done for us– as the gift of sight pertains to present events– what God is now doing for us. For example, your memory connects your consciousness to the invisible world of the past, as your sight connects your consciousness to the visible world of the present. When you are consciously connected to the past through your memory- coupled with the clarity and freshness of immediate experience through the power of the imagination- you can be moved emotionally by the experience of past events, just as you are moved by the experience of present events through the sight of such unfolding events. Therefore, no doubt as you share the encounters of these men of God, you will experience touching moments while sharing their experience. These moments will be unforgettable and will leave an indelible impression upon you. Indeed, such touching moments could prove to be teaching moments. As a result, your understanding and appreciation of these biblical accounts will be greatly enhanced and augmented by the power of your imagination.

On your spiritual odyssey through the Bible, you will embark on a timeless adventure of the soul. Your timely visits to the past to experience supernatural encounters will undoubtedly prove to be enlightening and spiritually uplifting. However, perhaps even more enlightening and spiritually uplifting will be the timely visit to the future. In the last chapter of A Spiritual Odyssey, you will make a timely visit to a future time– to the time of the Rapture. As you are mentally transported to the time of the Rapture, you will experience the wonder of wonders– the glorious Rapture– when all true believers are taken up to heaven to be with Jesus forever.

As it was mentioned before, It is absolutely necessary to be spiritually prepared, before taking your mental journey through time. You can prepare yourselves spiritually by doing the following:

First, you must not only read about the account of the events, which are described in the Bible, but you must truly believe that these events have actually occurred.

Secondly, you need to meditate on these events, while praying that the Holy Spirit will guide your imagination so that the images in your mind are not merely figments of your vain imagination, but mental images inspired by the

Holy Spirit. Indeed, it is possible for you to know when the Spirit of Truth is really guiding you. If you feel drawn closer to God, and feel that you are in his presence by your mental journey through time, then this would be a clear sign that your mental journey has become essentially a spiritual journey, and that the Spirit is guiding you; indeed, the Holy Spirit always draws you closer to God.

Thirdly, you should prepare yourself by focusing your mind on the time and place of your destination in the past as it is presented in the Bible. Focusing your mind entails opening the mind's eye of your imagination to vividly see people, places and things, relative to biblical events in the distant past.

If you believe, meditate, and focus, on the biblical accounts of momentous events, then by the power of the Holy Spirit and through the guidance of the Word you will be mentally transported to biblical times with the speed of thought. In the twinkling of an eye, you will find yourself at the time and place of the biblical event– certainly not in body, but in mind, and spirit.

Hopefully, your timely visits to share the supernatural encounters of the Bible will be a learning experience for you. At the end of every chapter of your timely visits, you will be led to review some of the lessons that you have learned from your spiritual odyssey to biblical times, before moving on to the next chapter in your mental journey through time.

It seems evident that the response of readers to this book, will be largely based on their measure of faith in God's Word. Therefore, it is fervently hoped that the Holy Spirit will increase the measure of faith in every reader, who reads "A Spiritual Odyssey." This book has one purpose and one purpose only: To help each reader see Christ more clearly, love him more dearly, and follow Him more nearly. Hopefully, every reader will have the desire to truly know God, and to become one with God through Christ Jesus.

Timely Visit with Abraham, the Intercessor: You Are There

The following is based on the account of the life of Abraham that can be found in Genesis 18:1-33.

"My Lord, if now I have found favor in thy sight pass not away, I pray thee, from thy servant."
Genesis 18:3

Prepare yourself to enter the time machine of your mind to become a time traveler of the Bible. Let your mind, enlightened by the Holy Scriptures and guided by the Holy Spirit, transport you to the time of the patriarch, Abraham, the father of God's chosen people, the Jews. The time of your mental visit to the past will coincide with a most extraordinary and momentous event. You will be there to witness the event when according to the

Bible, God in the flesh visited Abraham at his home, and ate a meal prepared by Abraham.

The Bible reveals that God in the flesh visited Abraham while he was sitting in the heat of the day before his tent. Abraham's home was then located on the plains of Mamre, not far from the city of Sodom. Read and meditate on the account of this event, which is so graphically described in Genesis chapter 18.

After reading the account of Abraham's encounter, prayerfully ask the guidance of the Holy Spirit. Always remember when you take this kind of journey that without divine guidance, your imagination will be nothing more than a vain imagination, full of sights, sounds, and surreal sensations but signifying nothing in terms of spiritual value. However, as you have no doubt experienced so far, when your imagination is directed by the word of God and guided by the Spirit, your mental journey will be more than just meaningless mental images. You could personally experience a divine encounter through the Holy

Spirit, who enlightens the mind while he touches the depths of the soul.

Now just imagine. Imagine the time, long ago, and the place– Abraham's dwelling– not too far from the city of Sodom. What do you see through the eyes of your imagination? Do you see the smoke from an altar of sacrifice as it rises high above Abraham's tent? The smoke from the altar fills the air with the pleasant aroma of a sacrificed animal's roasting flesh; the cloud of smoke from the altar of sacrifice is drifting in the wind toward Sodom. And do you see Abraham, with his long hair and beard, white as snow, as he sits in front of the large doorway of his tent? Take a closer look inside the tent. Do you also see his wife, Sarah, stooped with age, sitting near the back of the tent, fanning with a large fan in the heat of the day? Turn around now and look at the land surrounding the tents of Abraham and his servants. Can you see his servants in the distance on the wide, grassy plains tending a large herd of cows while other servants are tending even larger herds of sheep and goats on a far hillside? Do you hear the children of the servants laughing while playing, and do you also hear the bleating of the sheep and the goats and the lowing of the cattle grazing on the plains of Mamre?

The sights and sounds and smell of Abraham's dwelling now surround you. The sound of the gleeful laughter of the children is everywhere like the sweet aroma from the altar of sacrifice and the smoke rising high above Abraham's peaceful and serene looking homestead. Touch down, you are here! The year is 1898 BC. You have just arrived at the time when Abraham is about to be visited by God in the physical form of God in the flesh, who is known as the Son of God, Israel's future Messiah.

Abraham's Guests

Standing under a large tree– less than fifty feet from where Abraham is seated near the door of his tent– you can see quite clearly the kindly looking, weather-beaten face of the old patriarch. He has reached a venerable age; at this time in his life, he is about ninety years old. But the vitality in his demeanor and the sharpness and alertness in his soft blue eyes belie his venerable age. He is looking out into the distance; so you turn your eyes to look in the direction of his gaze.

Abraham's eyes are focused on the steep mountainside high above his dwelling. Squinting as he looks in the direction of the sun, he places his hand above his eyes to shield them from the glaring sunlight. Looking upward, you find yourself also squinting in the bright sunlight. In the distance, high on the mountainside, you barely can see three figures descending. Abraham is watching them with keen interest as they cautiously climb their way down the steep mountainside toward his dwelling, situated near the foot of the mountain on the plains of Mamre. After descending the steep mountainside, the three men move quickly over the level ground of the plains. They are heading straight toward Abraham's dwelling.

As they approach Abraham's tent, you can see that two of the men are quite young, perhaps in their late twenties, while the other is much older– his hair and beard white with age. This impressive-looking personage, with a thoughtful and pensive expression etched on his face, carries a shepherd staff in his hand. One of the two young men is wearing a dark blue mantle; on his face, he wears a grave, brooding countenance. This young man and the older man is following close behind the one who appears to be their leader. The young man, who is walking in the lead, has nothing in his hands and is dressed in a very simple manner. However, his demeanor– walking erectly with head held high– is like that of a man with authority.

Abraham's face is suddenly framed with a look of recognition. His countenance beams with sublime ecstasy as he leaps from his chair. Excitedly, but in deep reverence, with head bowed low, he races to meet the three figures as they approach. Reaching them, he falls on his knees, bowing his head toward the ground as he says in a voice high pitched and quivering with excitement, "My Lord, if now I have found favor in your sight, pass not a way, I pray you, from your servant."

The man, whom Abraham addressed as "My Lord," smiles serenely and looks down compassionately upon the kneeling patriarch with tenderness reflected in his eyes. His demeanor reflects simultaneously the authority of a king and the humility and tenderness of a close and a deeply affectionate friend. He exudes a most gracious demeanor, indeed.

Reflecting now on the biblical account of this event in Genesis, there is no doubt in your mind that you are standing with Abraham in the divine presence of God visiting the father of the Jewish people in the flesh. The scripture specifically says that "The Lord (YHUH) appeared unto him in the plains of Mamre" (Genesis 18:1). In the Hebrew translation, Lord means "Yahweh or Jehovah," which is the name of God. Clearly, Yahweh, who is about to be fed by Abraham, is not a vision. Also,

Yahweh is not in the form of an angelic being, or a spiritual entity, but in the form of a man made of flesh and blood.

Now your mind is suddenly flooded with questions, each question leading to another. Of course most Bible scholars would agree that it is certainly possible for the Son of God to be seen in the flesh, thousands of years before he came to the earth, but only as the pre-incarnate Son of God– not the incarnate Son of God. However, is it also possible that Jesus, as God incarnate, traveled back through time from the future to the time of Abraham, like Moses and Elijah traveled several hundred years from the past to the time of Christ? And if so, could Moses and Elijah, who were both seen with Jesus at the time of his transfiguration, be the two men with him now? (Matthew 17:1-13)

Suddenly, you realize that certain mysteries are so mind boggling that it is impossible to wrap your mind around them. Indeed, one can only speculate about such mysteries, because in the spiritual realm we still must look through a "glass darkly." It is far better to focus on what you know-like the amazing love of God for mankind- than to focus on what you do not know for sure. The Bible says that when we get to heaven "we shall know, even as we are known." Although you may have an appetite or desire for the revelation of biblical mysteries, you are constrained to practice delayed gratification. So you can only wait upon the Lord for the revelation of such mysteries.

Abraham's Joy in Serving His Friend

Getting up from his kneeling position, Abraham, with the reverence of a servant but with the warm endearment of a friend, says, "Let a little water, I pray you, be fetched, and wash your feet, and rest yourselves under the tree yonder."

He escorts the three men to the large, shady tree in front of the tent, where you have been standing, observing his meeting with the three men. He then signals his servants to bring out mats on which his guests can sit and rest. When they are comfortably seated, he says, "I will fetch a morsel of bread, and you will comfort your hearts. After that you shall pass on, for therefore, are you come to your servant."

The three men nodded appreciatively. The one, whom Abraham addressed as "My Lord," replies in a warm tone, "So do, as you have said."

You follow after Abraham as he walks with great haste toward his tent. Entering the tent behind Abraham, you find Sarah still fanning herself in the heat of the day. Sarah's face is pleasantly round with deep dimples; her skin, smooth and soft without a trace of wrinkle. Indeed, she seems incredibly well preserved. The budding beauty of youth has been replaced with another kind of beauty: The exquisitely dignified beauty of growing old gracefully. Her silver-gray hair is remarkably long, cascading over her shoulders.

Abraham says to Sarah, with a voice raised to a high pitch, betraying his great excitement, "Make ready quickly three measures of fine meal, knead it, and make cakes upon the hearth."

Before Sarah can respond, he quickly turns around and darts out of the tent. She slowly gets up from her seat, with the effort and caution of one who has long past her prime. She stands there, momentarily frozen, looking stupefied. Then walking across the large tent to the doorway, she peeps out. She sees the three men sitting comfortably under the large shady tree and conversing together. Sudden recognition widens her eyes; a deep reverence washes over her face as she fastens her eyes upon the Lord. With a burst of energy, she quickly turns away from the doorway to carry out her husband's instructions.

Standing at the doorway of the tent, you watch Abraham as he runs into a herd of cattle. He seems to be searching among the herd to find a special calf. He calls out to his servant- a young man, standing close by. "I have found one without any blemish, tender and good for my Lord. Here, take this calf. Make haste to cook and dress it."

With his face beaming with ecstasy, he dances his way back to the tent even as he hurries at the same time to prepare the meal for his guests. Hearing Abraham's instructions to his servant about "dressing the calf for eating," you realize that he is providing much more than just the morsel of bread, which he promised his guests. He is about to make a feast for his three guests.

Watching the joy and excitement of Abraham, the understanding of this scripture now becomes clear to you when Jesus remarked to the Jews concerning his loving relationship with the patriarch, "Abraham rejoiced to see my day, and he saw it and was glad." (John 8:56) No wonder the Jews were so puzzled by this statement. As far as they were concerned, Jesus was making himself to be like God. They asked, how could he have visited Abraham? They even took up stones to stone Jesus. Indeed, at that time, the unbelieving Jews could never envision Jesus visiting Abraham as the pre-incarnate Son of God or– admittedly this is purely speculative– as the divine time traveler, the incarnate Son of God.

Sarah's Unbelief

Within a very short time, a table laden with food is placed under the large, shady tree where the three visitors are seated. There are cakes made from fine meal as well as butter, milk, and meat from the fatted calf, which Abraham introduces to his guests as "tender and good." Abraham leans against the tree and watches with obvious satisfaction his three guests eating heartily the meal that he has prepared for them. While the Lord is eating the cake, which Sarah baked, he asks, "Where is Sarah your wife?"

Turning and nodding his head toward the tent, Abraham says, "Behold, in the tent."

The Lord takes another cake. But this time he spreads a copious amount of butter on the cake before eating it with obvious relish. While eating, he pauses to look up at Abraham, a tender expression framing his face, and he says, "I will certainly return unto thee according to the time of life, and, lo, Sarah thy wife shall have a son."

Abraham's face beams with a joyous response of deep gratitude. It is clear to you that as far as Abraham is concerned, if the Lord says it, he believes it, and that settles it. The Lord pauses again for a moment, tilting his head as if carefully listening. Then he asks Abraham in a plaintive voice that reverberates with his deep concern, "Wherefore does Sarah laugh saying, 'Shall I of a surety bear a child, when I am old?' Is anything too hard for the Lord? At the time of thy appointment I will return unto thee, according to the time of life, and Sarah shall have a son."

Sarah's face can now be seen protruding from the door of the tent. It is evident that she heard the Lord's statement about her laughter. Abraham and his guests turn to look at her as she slowly and shyly walks over to Abraham, where he is leaning against the tree. Sarah's eyes are cast down toward the ground, her face marred with a guilty expression. Her demeanor seems to reflect at once trepidation and guilt.

With eyes still cast down, unable to face the Lord, she says, "I laughed not."

The Lord, looking tenderly on Sarah, says ruefully, "Nay, but you did laugh."

It seems clear to you that Sarah does not have the faith of Abraham and does not share the same relationship with the Lord as her husband. She appears stiff and self-conscious as she stands before the Lord. It is obvious that she is afraid to express her doubt and skepticism to the Lord, so she denied laughing at his promise that she would have a child. You begin to wonder about your own faith; doubting is so easy when you leave the power and love of God out of the existential equation. You find yourself empathizing with doubtful Sarah, because certainly you have been there and done that.

You are realizing now for the first time that perhaps the reason for doubts and fears is due to the meager measure of one's love for God. The correlation between love and faith seems only too evident. To have the faith of Abraham, you must love God like Abraham. Unlike Sarah, Abraham is a friend of God, because he is absolutely convinced of God's unconditional love for him. So he believes, without a shadow of doubt, that nothing is too hard for his divine friend to do for him, because the Lord cares so much for him. Oh, if you could only love Jesus like Abraham! If God said it, then you would believe it, and indeed, that would settle it.

Sarah, hearing the Lord's gentle rebuke about her doubts, nervously lifts her downcast eyes to look upon the Lord. And the warm, tender love and compassion reflected in his eyes at once melted away her fear. As fear melts away, faith in the Lord's promise begins to take shape. Then her heart feels the sudden stabbing pain of remorse, and tears of repentance gushes from her eyes.

Broken and contrite she says, "Lord forgive my doubting heart."

Abraham and his guests are moved by the tearful Sarah standing before them. But through her tears, a smile breaks out on her face as she sees the smiling face of the Lord. Seeing his smiling face brings instant reassurance to Sarah- all is forgiven; all is well when God shines his smiling face upon you. Abraham reaches out his hand to his wife. Sarah moves toward him and is enfolded in the loving embrace of her husband.

Abraham's Attempt to Intercede

Standing beside the tree close to Abraham and Sarah, you watch as Abraham's guests prepare to take their leave. The Lord gets up from the table and walks over to where Abraham is embracing Sarah. The other two guests, whom you suspect- you just can't shake this feeling- could be Moses and Elijah, now get up from the table to follow the Lord. Seeing both men standing there with the Lord, you remember how they were standing together on the Mount of Transfiguration with the Lord Jesus, when Peter declared, "Lord, it is good for us to be here. Let us build three tabernacles: one for thee, one for Moses and one for Elijah." However, there is little doubt in your mind that the

Lord– whether the pre-incarnate Lord, or the incarnate Lord– is none other than Christ, the Lord.

The Lord places his hand on Abraham and Sarah, blessing them, and then he repeats his promise to them: "At the time appointed, I will return unto you, according to the time of life, and Sarah shall have a son."

Sarah laughs again. But this time, the Lord is laughing with her. Now everyone joins in the laughter. It is clear to everyone that her laughter is not the laughter of skepticism or unbelief, but the laughter of unbridled joy, the joy of being able to experience life in her womb, when all hope was gone Faith has now replaced doubt in the heart of Sarah. How true, indeed; hope springs eternal.

You watch as the three guests express their heartfelt gratitude to Abraham and Sarah for their hospitality. The tender loving bond that exists between the hosts and their guests is evident to you, and quite touching. Biding good-bye to Abraham and Sarah, the three guests take their leave, turning to go in the direction of Sodom.

But Abraham follows them, expressing his wish to go part of the way with them. Desiring to see more of Abraham's interaction with the Lord, you follow after them; your curiosity reaching a fever pitch. However, more than anything else, you follow after them, because of the sheer joy of being in the presence of the Lord. The joy of hearing his words, and seeing the embodiment of grace and truth on this spiritual odyssey of the mind is truly the kind of joy that is unspeakable and is without measure.

Turning to two men who are following him, the Lord says, "Shall I hide from Abraham the thing that I do, seeing that Abraham shall surely become a great and mighty nation, and all the nations of the earth shall be blessed in him? For I know that he will command his children and his household after him, and they shall keep the way of the Lord to do justice and judgment that the Lord may bring to Abraham that which he hath spoken of him."

Both men gravely nod their heads in agreement, trusting in the infallible judgment of the Lord. Abraham turns to look on the Lord with a questioning look on his face.

The Lord's face is now etched with deep sadness as he addresses his friend. He says, "Because the cry of Sodom and Gomorrah is great, and because their sin is very grievous, I will go down now and see whether they have done altogether according to the cry of it, which is come unto me, and if not I will know."

Abraham comes to a sudden halt on the road. He seems speechless. He appears to be terribly shaken by the news of God's pending judgment on Sodom and Gomorrah. The reason for such an expression of alarm from Abraham is revealed in the biblical account of the destruction of the twin cities. There is a considerable number of people living in Sodom and Gomorrah. If the cities were to be destroyed, there would be a great loss of lives. But in addition to this consideration, Abraham has a personal stake in Sodom: His nephew, Lot, and his family live in Sodom. No doubt, at this moment Abraham is terribly worried about Lot and his family.

Seeing the deeply troubled look upon Abrahams face, the Lord also comes to a halt. He appears to be quite concerned for his friend, Abraham. He beckons for the two men to continue on their journey to Sodom while he stands silently in the middle of the road with his friend, waiting to hear his response. Still speechless, Abraham stands in the middle of the road, looking extremely anxious and forlorn. He holds his head with both hands, agonizing over the shocking news of God's pending judgment upon Sodom and Gomorrah.

While standing there with the Lord and Abraham, you watch as the two men, who were with The Lord, wend their way toward Sodom and Gomorrah. Again, you find yourself wondering if these two men are angels, appearing with the pre-incarnate Son of God. Or on the other hand, could they be really Moses and Elijah, now appearing with the incarnate Son of God in the time of

Abraham, as they once appeared with him on the Mount of Transfiguration? Certainly, one could argue that the sign and wonder of fire and brimstone raining down from heaven on the evil cities of Sodom and Gomorrah suggest the modus operandi of these two prophets. According to the Bible, Moses and Elijah brought destruction upon evil doers by performing signs and wonders–Moses bringing destruction to the Egyptians, and Elijah destruction to idol worshipers in Israel.

Once again you recoil from the possibility that this could be an overly speculative thought on your part. God forbid that you should indulge in any vain imagination. And so you pray now: Dear Lord, guide my thoughts by your Holy Spirit. Please let me always be cognizant of the fallibility of my thoughts and my imagination. If my imagination, now is wondering away from the truth, please keep it in check. Lord, give me the wisdom to know the difference between speculation, and divine revelation. In Jesus name, I pray this prayer.

Again, you open the eyes of your imagination to view Abraham's encounter with the Lord. He moves closer to God, in the flesh, who is patiently waiting for his friend to speak. These words of Abraham in the Bible now echo through the canyons of your mind:

He says with a voice shaken with emotion, "Wilt thou also destroy the righteous with the wicked? Peradventure there are fifty righteous within the city, wilt thou also destroy and not spare the place for the fifty righteous that are therein? That would be far from thee to do after this manner, to slay the righteous with the wicked, and that the righteous should be as the wicked, that would be far from thee. Shall not the judge of the earth do right?"

You can see how the painful expression on Abrahams face is mirrored on the face of the Lord. He seems to be feeling Abraham's pain. He answers, "If I find in Sodom fifty righteous within the city, then I will spare the entire place for their sakes."

Abraham smiles, as if he sees a ray of hope. He says, "Behold now, I have taken upon me to speak unto the Lord which I am but dust and ashes. Peradventure, there shall lack five of the fifty righteous, wilt thou destroy the entire city for lack of five?"

The Lord says gravely, "If I find there forty and five, I will not destroy it."

Abraham says again, "Peradventure there shall be forty found there."

The Lord answers, "I will not do it for forty's sake.

"Abraham, now smiling broadly, says, "Oh, let not the Lord be angry, and I will speak. Peradventure there shall thirty found there?"

Looking compassionately on his friend, he replies, "I will not do it if I find thirty there.

With his hope increasing with every answer from the Lord, Abraham says, "Behold now I have taken upon me to speak unto the Lord: Peradventure there shall be twenty found there?"

Once again, Abraham's persistence in asking seems to elicit a gracious response from the Lord: "I will not destroy it for twenty's sake."

Abraham says, "Oh, let not the Lord be angry, and I will speak yet but this once: Peradventure ten shall be found there." Responding with the same patience and gracious manner to his friend's passionate intercession for Sodom and Gomorrah, the Lord says gravely, I will not destroy it for ten's sake."

The Lord stands before his friend quietly waiting, as if expecting to hear a continuation of the patriarch's impassioned intercession on behalf of the people living in the twin cities. It seems that the Lord's boundless grace for sinners is conditioned on the faith of Abraham, the intercessor. He stands in the road leading to Sodom and Gomorrah patiently waiting to hear more from Abraham. But Abraham pauses, and turns to look across the wide plains in the direction of Sodom.

The two men (Angels? or Moses and Elijah?) can still be seen far away in the distance on their way to Sodom. He turns to face the Lord again, but now he seems tentative, uncertain. Gesturing with his hand, he starts to say something, but then he hesitates, abruptly dropping his hands to his side. He seems torn. Apparently, Abraham now has doubts about how much more he can ask his divine friend. And his passionate appeal comes to an abrupt end, like an inflated balloon suddenly losing air.

Listening to Abraham's passionate prayer to God to spare the souls of Sodom and Gomorrah, you are now left with mixed emotions. You are feeling both impressed and distressed at the same time. You are certainly impressed by Abraham's passion and fervor in his intercession to God, but you are feeling some distress at his failure to continue interceding, in view of the Lord's willingness to grant every request that he made. It seems to you that he has suddenly placed a limit to God's grace by limiting his request. Does not the

Bible say, "Where sin abounded grace did much more abound?" There is absolutely no doubt in your mind that the amazing grace of God would exceed the sins of every sinner in Sodom and Gomorrah, if only Abraham had more faith in God's grace.

Suddenly, the reason why Abraham relented in his request dawns upon you, as his words echo in your mind: "Shall not the judge of the earth do right?" There was no cry for God's mercy from Abraham. It seems to you that Abraham was more focused on justice than grace. He was not pleading for God's grace, which has no limit, but he was pleading for God's justice to be tempered with the consideration of the inherent goodness of mankind.

Apparently Abraham was trusting in the righteousness of some of the citizens of Sodom and Gomorrah to save the rest of the people, who were corrupted by sin. But there were not ten righteous persons in the twin cities. The Bible reveals that even Lot and his family were corrupted by the sin of Sodom. Lot and his family escaped the destruction of Sodom, because the Lord remembered the righteousness of Abraham.

Apparently, as far as Abraham was concerned, justice that is tempered with mercy has its limits. In his mind it would take at least ten righteous person to become the "salt" of Sodom and Gomorrah to preserve them from the corruption and the destruction of sin. However, grace which is unmerited and undeserved has no limit. No doubt this gift of grace would have been freely given by the gracious Lord. Through the grace of repentance, all the people could have been saved.

Believing that the inherent goodness of mankind will ultimately prevail, Abraham now falls down on his knees before the Lord. You can hear him uttering words of thanksgiving, thanking the Lord for granting his requests. As Abraham is speaking with his head bowed before the Lord, a sorrowful expression envelops the Lord's countenance. He extends his hands over Abraham in a gesture of blessing him, then he turns to look in the direction of Sodom. At that moment the Lord disappears, vanishing into thin air.

When Abraham stops praying, he looks up to see the empty space where God in the flesh was standing. But he shows no sign of surprise. It occurs to you that no doubt Abraham has had other encounters like this before, when his divine friend suddenly vanishes into thin air.

Abraham's Misplaced Trust

Looking on Abraham's troubled countenance, you can just imagine how his heart is now torn with anxious feelings about his beloved nephew and family. Your heart goes out to him as he heaves a deep sigh while he gazes across the plains toward Sodom and Gomorrah. Now the setting sun is about to sink below the horizon. Soon darkness will fall. Turning around, with an anxious look on his face, Abraham begins to walk back home. And you follow.

You are simply amazed at the remarkable strength and agility of the ninety-year-old patriarch. You find yourself almost running to keep up. You are sweating profusely while walking at his fast pace. Then he suddenly stops and turns around to look back in the direction of Sodom. He stands in the road transfixed with deep concern etched on his face; rigid and unmoving he stands for a long moment, with eyes searching the horizon. Everything seems quiet and peaceful in the distance. The sun is slowly disappearing beyond the horizon. With a hopeful expression on his face, he becomes less rigid, and his taut face seems more relaxed.

He continues to walk on his way home, but now he is walking more slowly. Looking down on the ground as he walks, unmindful of the surroundings, he seems to be in deep thought. You wonder what he is thinking about. Could it be that he is thinking about the way he negotiated with the Lord on behalf of Sodom and Gomorrah? Is he feeling some uneasiness in placing his trust in the righteousness of ten Sodomites to save the cities from destruction? Perhaps he is no longer certain as he was before, that there are at least ten righteous persons living in Sodom and Gomorrah. It just could be that he is realizing now that he has placed too much trust in the righteousness of men.

God's Justice Condemns, but His Grace Forgives

While following Abraham on his way home, disturbing questions again begin to trouble your mind. Again you wonder, why did Abraham stop in his negotiation after the Lord readily agreed to withhold God's judgment on the basis of ten righteous persons living in Sodom and Gomorrah? It seems possible that God would have spared the city even if there were less than ten righteous persons living there.

You just can't get the thought out your mind that if God so mercifully agreed to lower the required number of the righteous for the prevention of divine judgment, from fifty to ten righteous persons, would he not also agree to lower such requirement from ten to nine...to eight...to seven...to six...to five...to four...to three...to two...or to one or even to none? Certainly, there was no sign that Abraham was exhausting God's willingness to withhold his judgment. Abraham did not really determine how far God would go to spare the twin cities; he negotiated with the Judge of the earth, but failed to seek the amazing grace of the Redeemer. Because of such amazing grace, the Lord at a future time would die for the sins of the world.

The Lord's gracious response to Abraham's negotiation should not really be surprising to you, because wherever you find Jesus– God in the flesh– you find the manifestation of God's grace. Again the word of God comes to your mind: "Where sin abounded, grace did much more abound," through Christ Jesus. There is no question that sin abounded in Sodom and Gomorrah, but because the Son of God was present at that time and in that place, grace did much more abound there. Because of God's abundant grace, Jesus says, "Ask and you shall receive, seek and you shall find, knock and it shall be opened unto you." Indeed, Abraham asked, but he limited his request. He sought, but he did not go far enough. He knocked, but he did not walk through the open door of grace.

Again the bothersome thought comes to your mind that Abraham placed too much trust in the righteousness of men and too little trust in God's grace. This thought simply will not leave your mind: Perhaps if Abraham had trusted in God's abundant grace as Savior instead of trusting in the righteousness of ten persons to satisfy the justice of the righteous Judge, the people of Sodom and Gomorrah would have been saved from destruction through repentance, like the wicked people of Nineveh. Certainly, there were no righteous persons in the great city of Nineveh, but through his grace and mercy God saved them all.

Suddenly, you recall from the Bible what Jesus had to say about the destruction of Sodom and Gomorrah. Jesus says, "If such miracles (God's

43

grace) had been seen in the wicked city, Sodom, it would have remained." (Matthew 11:23) Consider this stunning revelation by Jesus, God in the flesh, with whom Abraham negotiated! If Abraham had interceded as the messenger of the saving miracle of God's grace by preaching repentance to the people of Sodom and Gomorrah like Jonah preached to the people of Nineveh, they would not have been destroyed. You thank God for this revelation in the Scripture: God's amazing grace is boundless. Certainly, this thought is not just speculation. It is indeed, a revelation!

The Rising of One, the Falling of Another

Abraham quickens his pace as dusk begins to descend. It occurs to you that he is hurrying to return home to Sarah, who perhaps did not know about his intention to accompany his guests so far on their way to Sodom. Perhaps she might even now be waiting anxiously, wondering what has happened to him. Following closely behind Abraham, who is now walking briskly along the road that meanders around clumps of trees, you see in the distance lamp lights shining from the large tent of Abraham, surrounded by other lights from the numerous smaller tents of his servants.

As you move closer toward his impressive-looking homestead, you see Sarah standing before the doorway of the tent, watching her husband as he approaches. Seeing her standing there, Abraham begins to walk even faster toward his wife who seems to have been anxiously waiting for him. She begins moving toward him as he approaches her, with both arms extended. They hug each other passionately like lovers that have been too long separated from each other.

It is obvious to you that despite their advanced age, the flame of romantic love is still burning. As you watch the two lovers hugging and then entering their tent together, the thought occurs to you that tonight could be the rise of one people, while it could be the fall of another. Did not the Lord just promise a little while ago that Sarah would now conceive and have a son?

On another meeting with Abraham, God also promised that through his son a mighty nation would come. It is possible that tonight, Sarah could conceive. Tonight could be the beginning of the mighty nation promised by God; tonight, God's amazing grace in blessing all people through the seed of Abraham could begin through Sarah's conception. Yes, tonight could be the night of God's grace to the world; the beginning of God's chosen people, through whom, God, will take on flesh to dwell among mankind. But tonight also is the night of God's justice; the fall of another people, the fall of the wicked and perverted cities of Sodom and Gomorrah.

Feeling tired from the long walk, you lean against the tree where Abraham prepared the feast earlier for his three guests. Reposing here, you begin to think about the coming events that Abraham will face tomorrow. It will be a most traumatic time for him.

The Bible reveals that on the following day after the visitation by the Lord, "Abraham woke up early in the morning, and came to the place where he had stood before the Lord." There, Abraham will find out the verdict of God: guilty or not guilty. From the vantage point at the place where he stood before the Lord, the Bible reveals that "Abraham looked toward Sodom and Gomorrah, and toward all the land of the plain, and beheld; and lo, the smoke of the country went up as the smoke of a furnace."

It is hard to imagine how Abraham will face the awful sight of so many lives going up in smoke, as he looks tomorrow morning across the plains toward Sodom and Gomorrah.

But joy will come when he learns that God in His mercy has saved his nephew Lot and his family by sending two angels to take them out of the fiery furnace of Sodom. And joy will come again when he holds his newborn son Isaac in his bosom.

As you contemplate the judgment of God, you remember the words of a famous evangelist: "If God withhold judgment from certain cities in our nation, he will have to apologize to Sodom and

Gomorrah." Indeed, unlike Sodom and Gomorrah, the message of repentance has been preached to the cities of our nation. But still, the perversion and wickedness in our world is so pervasive that one must wonder how long it will be before the same judgment of God fall not only upon this nation, but this world.

God's Plan of Salvation

Leaning against the tree beside Abraham's tent, you continue for a while to muse about the marvelous plan of God's salvation to save the fallen human race. With the fall of night descending and the darkness deepening, a myriad of twinkling stars now appear in the night sky. The biblical account of God' promise to Abraham once again comes to your mind: "As the stars of heaven are great in number, so will be your children."

When the light in Abraham's tent suddenly goes out, again the thought occurs to you that tonight could be the night of Sarah's conception of

Isaac– the beginning of a people who will be as numerous as the stars of heaven. Soon Isaac, the first "star" from the seed of Abraham will be born, and then ultimately the rise of God's chosen people with the knowledge of the one and only God, shining as innumerable points of light, reflecting the Father of Lights. The promised seed of Abraham will have a tremendous impact on the people of the world, who live in a world of darkness. Indeed, they shall become a light unto the Gentiles.

In time wise men from Gentile nations will come from the East to follow the star over Bethlehem. And they will be led by the Holy Spirit to the promised "seed of Abraham" where they shall find an everlasting blessing. In the fullness of time, all the Gentile nations of the earth will follow the Day Star from heaven. Indeed, the Wise men from Gentile nations will announce the first Christmas to the Jews, the children of Abraham, when they follow the star of Bethlehem– the star of the Son of David– to find the Jewish Messiah, Jesus, the Light of the World. And the world will never be the same again!

How truly amazing is the Lord! His awesome power, and his unfathomable wisdom are beyond comprehension. The amazing love of God that implemented such a marvelous plan for redeeming your soul and giving you eternal life is truly the wonder of wonders. God in his mercy sent Christ to the earth. He crossed over the barrier of eternity and perhaps even the barrier of time to consummate your salvation. And this plan started with God's promise to Abraham– the promise that from his "seed" all nations of the earth would be blessed. Feeling utterly unworthy of such love, you fall down on your knees and thank God for his amazing grace in restoring your soul. Once you were spiritually lost but now you are found, blind but now can see, and dead but now made alive in Christ Jesus.

Realizing that the time has now come to return from your mental journey, you decide to close the eyes of your imagination. And in the twinkling of an eye, you are transported back to the future- the present time. Here you are again, back from the past, and now fully conscious of the present, but still feeling the awesome presence of the Lord.

Indeed, the time machine of the mind, guided by the Spirit, has taken you further than you expected, far beyond just mere imagination. It is becoming evident to you that your mental journey through God's Word became a journey to a new dimension of spiritual understanding. As a believer in Christ- a seeker of the truth- you now pray that your mental journey to the time of Abraham will leave an indelible and a lasting impression, not only on your mind, but on your heart, and soul as well.

Lessons Learned in Odyssey

One lesson that should never leave our minds is the close friendship one can have with almighty God. God loves us no less than he loves Abraham, and we can share the same friendship with him, if we spend more time in the presence of our divine friend. Yes, God wants to be our friend. No one loves us like the lowly Jesus, no not one. Indeed, what a friend we have in Jesus! When we need him, he is always there. Our friend has promised to never leave us nor forsake us. Jesus, our precious friend died for us.

Still another lesson to be learned is that the amazing grace of God is only limited by our limited faith. As we now reflect on Abraham's intercession for the people of Sodom and Gomorrah, we can see how faith is the key that unlocks the door of grace. However, although Abraham was a man of faith, yet his faith set a limit to the boundless grace of God. When we pray to God, we should always remember Jesus' words: "with God nothing is impossible." Indeed, there is no limit to the grace of God. Therefore, we should never limit our faith in God.

Timely Visit with Abraham at Beer-Sheeba: You are There

The following is based on the biblical account of Abraham being tested by God. (Genesis 22)

God says to Abraham, "Take now thy son, thine only son, Isaac, whom you love and get thee into the land of Moriah, and offer him there for a burnt offering upon one of the mountains which I will tell thee of." (Genesis 22:2)

Just imagine! Let your mind become unfettered by the barriers of time or the distance of space. Soar on the wings of imagination and travel with the speed of thought through the dimension of space-time to a place far, far away, and a time long, long ago. Enlightened by the Word of God, and led by the Spirit, let your mind take you on a spiritual odyssey back to the time of Abraham.

Begin your spiritual odyssey by reading the biblical account about Abraham offering up his son, Isaac, as a sacrifice unto the Lord. After reading the Bible, prayerfully meditate on what you have just read. While meditating focus your mind on Abraham, his son Isaac, and their home at Beer-Sheba in the land of Canaan long ago. Now open the eye of your mind: Imagine the time and place. And with the speed of thought, in the twinkling of an eye, you are traveling mentally to the past about four thousand years ago. You are arriving at the home of Abraham, one of the richest men in his time. Your arrival is just before his encounter with God in the year 4000BC. Here you are now. You have arrived!

Abraham's Homestead

It is night time, about an hour before the break of dawn. There is a bright moon shining above. You find yourself standing on a beaten path that meanders through a cluster of tents, directly ahead of you. The size of the tents are relatively small, and they are evenly spaced apart; more than likely this is the dwelling place of Abraham's servants. Far in the distance to the right of this sizable coterie of tent dwellers, you can see a large herd of cattle in the valley below. No doubt, Abraham's livestock. On the left on higher ground overlooking the tents you also see herds of sheep and goats on the hillside. Abraham's impressive homestead, with the numerous tents of his servants, is bathed in the splendor of the bright moon light.

You can hear the familiar night sound of crickets chirping, and you are greeted by the sound of roosters crowing, signaling the approach of morning. It is a calm, peaceful looking scene. But you know this is the calm before the storm: Abraham's encounter with God is about to take place.

You wonder where Abraham's tent is located in the midst of the cluster of tents. Then you notice an extremely large tent with a small tent adjacent to it, situated on a gentle slope overlooking the encampment. No doubt the large and imposing looking tent is where you will find Abraham and Sarah, his wife. Isaac will be in the small tent, adjacent to Abraham's tent.

Walking on the beaten path that meanders through the tent encampment, you then have to veer to the left in order to take a smaller path, leading up to the patriarchs' abode, the tents of Abraham and Isaac. A short distance from Abraham's tent there is a large tree, with a rock nearby, about three feet high. There you decide to sit on the rock and wait for a while for the expected coming events to unfold and to run their course. In the bright moon light you sit listening to the night sound of the cricket chirping and the roosters– like watchmen in the night– crowing with a trumpet-like sound to signal the approaching new day.

Your waiting is not long. Soon you see Abraham at the door of his tent, sliding away the curtain hanging before the door way, and then stepping out through the opening. He turns his head upward to gaze at the moon shining in all its splendor. Then he looks down toward the encampment of his servants, where the cluster of tents below is drenched in the warm moon glow. He yawns, stretching himself out with hands extended out from his sides, then rubs his eyes and face with his hand. He appears to be just waking up.

He now looks in the direction where you are seated on the rock, and immediately starts moving directly toward you. For a moment, as he is getting closer, it seems that he sees you. But that is simply not possible. You are here only in mind, not in body. And now you cannot help laughing at yourself as this amusing thought enters your mind: "I must be getting too carried away by my imagination." While Abraham is still heading toward where you are seated, you hurriedly get up from your seat on the rock, moving away over to the tree to stand there, leaning against it.

Abraham walks over to the rock, but he does not sit on it. He kneels before it. Kneeling before the rock, with hands placed on it as a means of support, he begins to pray. Indeed, you were using the rock as a seat, but for Abraham, the rock is more than just a seat. It is his altar of prayer. With eyes closed, he prays there quietly without uttering a word out loud.

Why? Why? Why?

While he is praying you are able to get a good look on the friendly looking, weather beaten face of the old patriarch. Abraham has reached the venerable age of a centurian; at this time he is well over a hundred years old. His long hair is as white as snow, and he has a long, flowing white beard. His face is lined with many wrinkles as his long life is graced with many years.

Noticing a sudden shadowing over his face, you look up to see a thick cloud passing over the moon, eclipsing its light. Soon everywhere is plunged into darkness. But Abraham with eyes closed takes no notice, and continues to pray. Then you hear the gentle rumbling of a voice, sounding like rolling thunder, "Abraham, Abraham!"

Abraham opens his eyes. He looks up toward heaven. He sees the dark cloud over the moon, the cloud now becoming a large pillar of cloud, looking dark and foreboding. He answers, "Behold here I am."

God says to Abraham, "Take now thy son, thine only son, Isaac, whom you love and get thee into the land of Moriah, and offer him there for a burnt offering upon one of the mountains which I will tell thee of."

Pause in time! At this point in your timely visit, you put your imagination on pause to reflect on the biblical account of this encounter with God.

There are absolutely no details given about Abraham's emotional reaction to the astounding commandment of God. The Bible seems to leave such details to your imagination. Certainly, Abraham would have been devastated and emotionally torn when he was commanded by God to sacrifice his son as a burnt offering. So, now through the eyes of your imagination, you begin to observe Abraham's reaction to the Lord's commandment. And what do you see?

You see Abraham's jaw dropping, his face now becoming ashen and taut by the shocking command of God. His eyes are open wide with a look of horror. He seems speechless. Before he can reply, the light of the moon suddenly reappears when the dark pillar of cloud covering the moon quickly disperses like smoke in the wind: A clear sign that his encounter with God has come to an abrupt end.

Looking above, Abraham sees the dark pillar of cloud quickly dispersing, and disappearing like smoke carried away by the wind. A look of indescribable agony is on his face as he turns to look toward Isaac's tent. You wonder what is going through the mind of Abraham at this moment in time. Is he feeling utterly confounded that the righteous and just God could command him to do such a dastardly deed? Does he believe that the sacrifice of his son is a consequence of the sins that he has committed? Is he thinking about how he can suppress his great love for his son, so that he can plunge a knife in his heart, or so that he can cut his throat to shed his blood as a sacrifice unto the Lord for the burnt offering?

Abraham places his hands on top of his head, and begins to shake his head wildly from side to side. Looking up to heaven, he cries out, his voice broken with deep anguish, Why? Why? Why Lord? Why?

His great agony seems unbearable. Still kneeling down before the rock, he now places both arms around it, hugging the rock close to himself. He is sobbing piteously, making loud, convulsive gasps. He moans over and over again, "O my son Isaac, O Isaac, my son, my son!" Tears coursing down his cheeks, his shoulders heaving with heart wrenching sobbing, he continues for a long while to repeat his mournful lament, "O my son, Isaac, O Isaac, my son, my son!"

The Connection Between Love and Obedience

As you watch Abraham's expression of grief for his son, grieving as if he were already dead, it seems clear to you that for him disobedience to God's commandment is not an option; his commitment to God is irrevocable. The only option for Abraham is complete obedience. Why such obedience? Because Abraham truly loves God. The Bible reveals that Abraham truly loved God with all his heart, with all his soul, with all his mind and with all his strength. According to Scripture, it is because of his great love for God why he was willing to sacrifice his son, his only son. So now you see that nothing, not even the strong, paternal love for his son, Isaac, can separate him from his God.

While you ponder the remarkable relationship that Abraham has with his creator, you begin to question the depth of your love for the Lord. God loves you no less than he loves Abraham. But are you returning his love? You wish you could answer in the affirmative. But to be honest, too often you have failed. You are suddenly realizing that God cannot be Lord at all, if he is not Lord over all.

After his mournful lament for his son, Isaac, he rises to his feet, looks up to heaven, reaches his hands upward and then closes his eyes in an attitude of prayer. His face is now framed with an expression of sublime peace and serenity. He prays silently, but based on the kind of expression that you see on his face, he is probably speaking to God in the language of an obedient servant right now, saying, "Not my will, but thy will be done." Indeed, every true servant prays to God with the attitude of humility: Their prayers are not really about changing the mind of God, but it is more about accepting the will of God. The good and faithful servant serves the Lord not from a sense of duty, but from a heart of love.

After praying, he turns to look at Isaac's tent once again. There is a curious expression on his face while he steadfastly looks in the direction of his son's tent. Turning to look also, you see a ram, appearing as white as snow in the moonlight, standing close to the door of Isaac's tent. Apparently, the ram wondered off from the herd further up on the hillside directly above the tents. Abraham gazes on the lamb with a puzzled expression on his face. No doubt he is wondering like you about the sudden appearance of the ram. Looking out to the east, he sees the faint light of dawn breaking over the horizon. Again he looks at the ram; then with a pensive look on his face, Abraham turns away to walk slowly over to his tent, and entering it, disappears from your view. But you know exactly what is now taking place behind the drawn curtain of Abraham's tent.

Based on the account of the Bible, you know that Abraham is right now proceeding at full speed to carry out God's command. His unquenchable desire to obey God is like a fire shut up in his bones. Soon he will be waking up Isaac. The Bible gives the following sequence of events: Early in the morning he will be getting up. He will first saddle his ass, and then he will wake up Isaac and two servants to go to the land of Moriah with him. He will ask his servants to cleave or split the wood for the burnt offering. After loading the wood for the burnt offering on the ass, Abraham, Isaac and his two servants will wend their way to the land of Moriah. Of course, Isaac, like a lamb going to the slaughter, will be clueless that he is the actual burnt offering.

No doubt at this moment, Abraham is hurriedly putting on his clothes, while extremely careful not to wake up his wife, Sarah. As he sees her sleeping, you wonder, what is going through his mind? Perhaps desperate thoughts are now whirling though his mind. You can imagine Abraham's anxious thoughts about his beloved wife. He is probably thinking these thoughts right now: "Sarah will have to know. But not now. This will kill her! It's like she's being sacrificed, too. Oh Lord! Provide a way."

You wonder if Abraham could ever share the Lord's command with his wife, Sarah. You just do not see how he could. After his incredible act of obedience, how could he tell her that the Lord commanded him to offer up their son as a sacrifice? How could he tell her that he had to kill their son? No doubt Sarah would think that Abraham was completely insane in his willingness to obey such a commandment. Sarah does not have the faith of Abraham, evidenced by her expression of unbelief when God told Abraham that he would give them a son in their old age. Based on Sarah's weak faith, you feel quite certain that she could never understand the depth of Abraham's love and obedience to the Lord.

God's Purpose for Testing His People

While reflecting on the possible reaction of Sarah, your attention is suddenly drawn to the strange appearance of the rock where Abraham was just praying. Sparkles of light can be seen on it; a strange kind of glitter near its top. Moving away from the tree on which you have been leaning, you walk over to the rock to get a closer look. As you look down on the smooth surface of the rock, saturated with Abraham's tears, the reason for the glittering rock is only too obvious: His tears are reflecting the light of the moon, becoming sparkles of light in the night.

And now suddenly you are experiencing a wonderful revelation. An epiphany! The revelation of this truth comes to you now with stunning clarity, as you consider all the great men of faith: God uses suffering and pain to shape, mold and transform his servants into sparkles of light that reflect his divine light, so that they can become the light of the world. The tears of pain and suffering are part of the molding process. At times God uses fiery trials to ignite the faith of believers so that they can shine like stars in the darkness of the world. As the light of the world they are called to lead those who are lost in darkness to Christ Jesus, the eternal light of heaven and earth.

While standing there looking down on the rock, sparkling in the moon light with Abraham's tears, it is so incredibly comforting to know that the all seeing eyes of God sees all your tears, and the loving heart of God feels all your pain, and the all knowing mind of God knows all your needs. When you truly know God who is your everlasting comfort, then despite your time of testing, you will experience lasting peace and serenity just like Abraham.

Indeed, you will have the peace that passes all understanding– peace in the storm. With this kind of peace, you will walk in the dark, and you will keep on walking when nothing makes sense. You will walk and not fall, because you walk by faith, and not by sight. Faith is the instinct of the soul that never reasons why, but will always do or die. Indeed the walk of faith is simply this: To trust and to obey. And as you trust and obey, God will empower you to pass every test that comes your way.

God Always Provides

Turning to look once again at the tents of Abraham and Isaac, you are surprised to see that the ram is no longer lying at the door of Isaac's tent; it is nowhere to be seen- nowhere on the hillside above and nowhere in the valley below. Its sudden disappearance is as mysterious as its sudden appearance a little while ago. Then you see a white form in the distance on the path leading away from Abraham's homestead. It is the ram. The ram is heading East.

Suddenly you remember the biblical account of the ram on Mount Moriah, when Abraham was about to offer up Isaac as a sacrifice. According to the Bible, the ram was found caught by its horns in a thicket, a dense growth of bushes. And the Lord accepted the ram as a burnt offering instead of Isaac.

You wonder: Could this be the same ram? This ram is heading East in the direction of Moriah. And Moriah is only three days journey from Abraham's dwelling. Could it be that God is leading this ram to Mount Moriah to be offered in the place of Isaac? Of course there can be no answer to this question, because the question is purely speculative. Now you are only imagining by your question what might be, not what has been revealed in God's Word. So one must always be careful to make the distinction between imagination and reality– the revealed truth. But this truth is clearly revealed in God's Word: The Lord always provides. And as the Lord provided for Isaac, he will provide for you.

Your thoughts turn to Jesus, and how God has provided the Lamb of God, who has taken away all our sins. The words of John 3:16 brings to you now a sweet solace: "For God so loved the world that he gave his only begotten Son that whosoever believes on him should not perish but have everlasting life." God's grace is truly amazing! He gave his son to die for our sins. God provided Jesus, his only begotten Son, as the Redeemer from sin, the anointed One, the Messiah, the Seed of Abraham through whom the world would be blessed.

And then you take one last look on Abraham's impressive homestead before taking your leave back to your time. But this timely visit to Abraham is to be continued. How you would like to witness Abraham's next encounter with God on Mount Moriah! However, first you must visit the time of Christ. Why? Because the incredible obedience of Abraham to God that you have just witnessed is really a precursor of Christ's obedience in the garden of Gethsemane. Indeed, it would be fascinating to compare both events.

Now you close the eyes of your mind, so you can no longer see the mental images of Abraham's homestead. And in the twinkling of an eye, with the speed of thought, you have traveled four thousand years through time. You are back now to your time. Your odyssey to this momentous event in the past is over, but the lessons you have learned will remain. And based on how you are feeling now, you are convinced that your journey through time was more than a mental journey. Indeed it was a spiritual journey, an amazing journey to glean spiritual gold nuggets from the past.

Lessons Learned in Odyssey

The parallel between the event on Mount Moriah and the event on Mount Calvary is mind boggling. Clearly, God ordained the offering of Isaac as a sacrifice to be a foreshadow of the sacrifice of Jesus, who is the Lamb of God. Just as Abraham was moved to sacrifice his son, because he loved God, God was moved to give his only begotten Son as a sacrifice for our sins, because he so loved us. However there is one noteworthy difference: God spared Abraham's son from death, but he did not spare his own Son from death. Christ Jesus died for our sins as the Lamb of God.

Our obedience to God is always connected to our love for him. Abraham obeyed God because he loved him. Jesus, said, "If you love me you will keep my commandments." God said to Abraham, "Now I know you love me, because you would sacrifice your son, your only son, for me." Loving God moves us to obey his will. True obedience is never motivated by fear. It is always motivated by love for God. Therefore, the Bible says that we should love the Lord with all our heart, mind, soul and strength.

Timely visit with Christ in the Garden of Gethsemane: You are There

"O my Father, if it be possible, let this cup pass from me; nevertheless, not as I will, but as thou wilt."

Matthew 26:39

Turn the pages of your imagination. Travel back to the time of Christ to witness his great agony in the garden of Gethsemane. It was there in the garden that Jesus began to pay the penalty for your sin that culminated on the cross with his triumphant cry, "It is finished!" Begin your spiritual odyssey by reading the biblical account of Jesus in the Garden of Gethsemane. Then meditate on the agonizing travail of Jesus in the garden, when the assailing forces of darkness attempted to thwart Jesus from fulfilling his mission for saving mankind. As a result of his unspeakable agony, Jesus sweat drops of blood.

Pray for spiritual guidance before you begin your mental journey. With the enlightenment of God's Word, and by the guidance of the Holy Spirit, you are now ready to spiritually embark on another timely visit to the time of Christ. Your spiritual odyssey through time will take you about two thousand years into the past- to the time of Christ.

As you prepare to leave, open the eyes of your imagination to see images of the time of Christ. Focus your mind on the Mount of Olives and the garden of Gethsemane that is located near the foot of the Mount of Olives. And in the twinkling of an eye, traveling at the speed of thought over two thousand years back to the past, you now arrive at the time of Christ.

Your arrival is on the night before his crucifixion. And the place of your arrival is on the summit of the Mount of Olives. From where you are, it is only about a ten minute walk down to the

Garden of Gethsemane. The time now is just about two hours before the arrest of Jesus by the solders of the Sanhedrin, the supreme religious body in the land of Israel.

The City of Jerusalem

Just like your timely visit to Abraham, you have entered the time of Christ during the night time. The radiance of the full moon illuminates the hillside of the Mount of Olives. The magnificent city of Jerusalem situated about two miles below the Mount of Olives can be seen in all its glory. You find the visual splendor of Jerusalem to be quite impressive.

The panoramic view of the city from the Mount of Olives is dominated by the gleaming, gold-embellished Temple which is located in the most holy place in all of Judea. Based on your research on this ancient city before taking this mental journey, you know that the location of the temple is the site of Mount Moriah, where Abraham offered up Isaac as a sacrifice almost two thousand years before the time of Christ. You can see the Temple standing high above the old city at the center of a gigantic white stone platform.

Also, based upon your research, you are able to distinguish the two sections of the city. You can see to the south of the temple, which is the location of The Lower City, a group of limestone houses, yellow-brown colored from years of sun and wind. In the moon light you can see very well the narrow, unpaved streets and houses that slope downward toward the valley, which runs through the center of Jerusalem.

To the west is the Upper City, called Zion, the dwelling place of the very rich. The white marble villas and palaces of the aristocratic or wealthy class are conspicuous in the moon light, and offers a sharp contrast to The Lower City. Two wide arched passageways span the valley, crossing over from the Upper City to the temple.

A tall, massive gray stone wall encircles Jerusalem. Viewing the city from the Mount of Olives, it appears that the wall around Jerusalem is at least three and a half miles in circumference.

You can see at intervals along the tall massive wall large gateways used by visitors to enter the city.

Standing on the summit of the Mount of Olives, you can also see the numerous olive groves that cover the mountain. The thought crosses your mind that no doubt many of the owners of the olive groves are the very rich residents living in The Upper City of Jerusalem, while their servants working in the olive groves live in The Lower City.

While gazing with wonder at the beautiful city of Jerusalem from the summit of the Mount of Olives, you momentarily forgot that Gethsemane, located at the foot of the Mount of Olives is your destination. So now you hurriedly begin to walk down the side of the Mountain. On your way down to the garden of Gethsemane, you wonder what the garden looks like. In many biblical accounts usually the description of persons, places and things are left to your imagination, because the details about such matters are just not given. Therefore, you feel that it behooves you to now use your imagination that is enlightened by the Word and guided by the Spirit.

Within a few minutes you reach a fairly large field, a grassy clearing, filled with wild flowers of all kinds. The lilies of the field are dancing in the breeze that is now blowing. There are lilies everywhere, perhaps the same lilies Jesus spoke about in his teaching of the disciples, when Jesus said to them: "Consider the lilies of the field," Jesus said to them, "they toil not, neither do they spin, yet I say unto you that even Solomon in all his glory was not arrayed as one of these." The small field is completely surrounded by olive trees. You immediately identify this place near the foot of the Mount of Olives to be the Garden of Gethsemane. Your attention is drawn to a narrow path leading up the hill side to the grassy clearing. Here in the moon light while leaning on an olive tree, you now wait for the arrival of Jesus with his disciples.

The Divinity and Humanity of Christ

While leaning against the olive tree, your thoughts turn to Jesus. You are here waiting to enter the presence of divinity. Jesus who is the Word that is made flesh is not only the Son of God, but he is God, the creator of the universe and the creator of all life forms, including mankind. You are feeling now so inadequate, so unworthy to enter the holy presence of Jesus, the Lord of lords and the King of kings, the almighty God.

The Bible teaches that God emptied himself of his power and glory, and took on flesh to become a man, when he was born as Mary's baby. Jesus, who is fully God and fully man, humbled himself as a servant, and came to the world to die for our sins. Wow! God's plan of redemption is absolutely mind boggling!

But what is equally mind boggling is that Jesus is also your friend. The almighty God is your friend! Why your friend? Because he loved you so, that he gave his life for you. On the one hand you are awed by his divinity, but on the other you are drawn to his humanity. And tonight, more than any time before, his humanity will be evident.

As you wait for the Lord, who is also your divine friend, to show up, you think about how he is probably feeling right now. Perhaps he is beginning to feel the crushing burden of sorrow, as the time of his crucifixion draws nearer; it is only a matter of hours now before he will be nailed to a cross. No doubt the passover supper earlier today–the last supper with his disciples–was extremely sad for him, and sad also for his disciples.

According to the Bible, in spite of his crushing burden of sorrow, he was moved to wash his disciples feet. Washing the twelve disciples feet after the passover supper is so indicative of his deep love and affection for them. It occurs to you now that he loves you no less; every day you experience his tender loving care. But too often such loving care goes unnoticed because of your callous human nature. So now as you watch for your friend to come walking up the Mount of

Olives you pray: Lord forgive me now; help me to love you like you love me.

And even as you are praying, you see Jesus coming toward you. In the moonlight you can see him walking up the mountain slope on the narrow path that meanders around the olive trees surrounding the Garden of Gethsemane. Following Jesus on the narrow path is a long line of men, his disciples, all walking close together in a single file.

When Jesus enters the Garden of Gethsemane, he stops and turns around to wait for the long line of disciples who are following. Soon everyone is gathered around Jesus. Raising up from your leaning position against the olive tree, you move closer to where they are gathered, so you can get a better view of Jesus. But he is now completely surrounded by his disciples, so you are unable to see him. You can see that there are only eleven disciples present in the garden, because Judas, who betrayed Jesus, is not there– at least not yet.

Based on the account of the Bible that is now guiding your imagination, you can identify Peter, the big fisher man; Andrew, his brother; James, the son of Zebedee; John, his brother; Phillip, the great evangelist; Bartholomew, Thomas, the doubter; Matthew, the tax collector; James, the son of Alphaeus; Thaddaeus, and Simon the Canaanite.

Through the eyes of your imagination, you are now looking on these men whom Jesus has chosen as his disciples.. They are all dressed in the traditional Jewish garb. Many of them are fisher men and all from humble beginnings; most lacking in training and education. Indeed, there is nothing remarkable about any of them. Yet through the preaching of the Gospel and the power of the Holy Spirit, this ragtag, motley group of men have changed the world forever. But tonight there is a shroud of gloom over these men. Their faces are enveloped with a look of profound melancholy.

The Travail of Jesus

When Peter, James and John, who are blocking your view, move a couple feet from the gathering to speak to each other privately, you turn your eyes to look upon Jesus. The moment that you behold the face of God in the flesh, your Savior from sin, tears gush from your eyes. You are now overcome with deep emotion: Jesus is about to pay the ultimate price for your sins. He is about to suffer and die for you! The sudden realization of his awesome love for you now overwhelms you, instilling a feeling of complete unworthiness, but at the same time you are experiencing such a feeling of gratitude that is beyond words.

His face is framed with exquisite sadness. Seeing the face of the Lord marred with such deep sorrow, the prophetic words of Isaiah suddenly echo through your mind: "He is despised and rejected of men, a man of sorrows and acquainted with grief." However, despite the dark shadow of gloom over his face and demeanor, there is deep compassion reflected in his eyes as he looks on his disciples. In a voice thick and heavy with emotion, Jesus says to them,

"Sit here while I go and pray, yonder."

The disciples, with a sad countenance on their faces, and looking weary and sleepy, one by one silently slump to the ground to sit and wait quietly for the Lord to have a time of prayer apart from them. Jesus then beckons Peter, James and John to go with him. You follow the three disciples as they walk with Jesus to the other side of the Garden of Gethsemane, but before reaching to the other side, he says to them,

"My soul is exceeding sorrowful, even unto death. Tarry ye here, and watch with me."

Peter, James and John appear to be as tired and sleepy as the rest of the disciples. Moving wearily over to a nearby rock in the grassy clearing, all three of them sit down, leaning their backs against the rock. For a moment you are feeling torn about what you should do: Should you accompany Jesus to the place where he is going to pray? Or should you stay here with the three disciples? You decide to stay with them, because obviously if you were here physically like the disciples, Jesus would require you to stay here as well.

While seated beside Peter, you watch the Lord as he goes a little further out into the Garden of Gethsemane. He is walking through a field of the most beautiful wild flowers that appear conspicuously radiant in the moon light. Then reaching to the place where a fairly large rock is lying, surrounded by wild flowers, he falls down on his knees beside it, and begins to pray. The appearance of the rock on which he is leaning is markedly different from the other rocks that you see in the garden. This oval shaped rock has a deep cleft on its side. The sound of his praying is within earshot of where you are seated, so you can hear his groaning and certain parts of his impassioned prayer fairly well.

You are overcome with emotion as you listen to his groaning that is filled with such indescribable agony. The emotional pain that the Lord is now feeling is only matched by the physical pain that he will be feeling soon, when he will be beaten mercilessly, and then nailed to a cross with a crown of thorns upon his head. Oh God, what a terrible price you must pay for my sin!

Jesus prays in a voice broken with deep emotion, "Abba, Father, all things are possible unto thee; take away this cup from me; nevertheless not what I will, but what thou wilt."

His prayer is followed with more groanings to the father. You suddenly realize that the cup of suffering that Jesus has to drink from goes beyond the pain and suffering on the cross. In fact his cup of suffering is far worse than the suffering on any cross or any physical pain. The cup that Jesus must drink from represents his spiritual suffering. The spiritual suffering of paying the penalty for the sins of the world is infinitely more painful than any physical suffering. Consider the spiritual suffering that Jesus is about to endure: The righteous Son of God must become sin, exchanging his righteousness for the sins of humanity, and be forsaken by the Father. The Son must be forsaken by the Father in order to reconcile sinners to the Holy God. And forsaken by the Father is the ultimate suffering: It is a living hell! This is the cup that Jesus must drink from. Such depths of suffering is unfathomable.

It is no wonder that as Jesus is praying right now, he is sweating drops of blood, because of the incredible intensity of his suffering. The bleeding does not start with the physical pain of his bruised and torn body; it starts with the horrific agony of his torn soul, the onslaught of the power of darkness to inflict pain, because Jesus is about to take upon himself the sins of sinful humanity. So, the Son will be forsaken by the Father whose holiness can have nothing to do with the sins that Jesus will bear on the cross. Such spiritual suffering is unimaginable! The bleeding of the holy Lamb of God for your sin starts now in the garden of Gethsemane, as Jesus sweats drops of blood.

The Weakness of the Flesh

While you are watching Jesus leaning on the rock, with his face resting on it as he is praying, you hear the sound of someone snoring. Turning around you find Peter, James and John fast asleep. You are mindful of the fact that Jesus specifically told them to stay here and watch with him. Well, so much for the weakness of the flesh. Then you hear footsteps approaching. You turn to see Jesus walking back. Oops! Now they are caught in the act.

Jesus walks over to the rock on which they are resting while sleeping, and gently shakes them by the shoulders to awaken them. He says to Peter, "Simon, sleepest thou? Couldest not thou watch one hour? Watch ye and pray lest ye enter into temptation. The spirit truly is willing, but the flesh is weak."

All three disciples, looking befuddled and embarrassed, mumbled expressions of remorse to the Lord. Jumping up, they frantically rub their eyes, and stretch out their hands to become fully awake. Nodding his approval for their effort to keep awake, Jesus returns to the place where he was praying. Peter, James and John sit down after a little while and settle themselves beside the rock just as before.

Again, you hear the same groaning from Jesus, the awful sound of indescribable agony. His voice, broken with deep anguish, can be heard repeating the same prayer as before, "Abba, Father, all things are possible unto thee; take away this cup away from me; nevertheless, not what I will, but what thou wilt."

As you listen to the prayer of the Lord, you are suddenly struck by the absolute necessity in having the right attitude when praying. The attitude should be selfless, not selfish. It should never be about what you want, but always about what God wants for you. Hence, Jesus prayed, "not what I will, but what thou wilt." You now remember that when Jesus taught his disciples how to pray, he told them to pray, saying, "Our Father, hollowed be thy name, thy kingdom come, thy will be done on earth as it is in heaven." Just as Jesus taught them to pray, saying "thy will be done," he is now praying the same way.

Once again, you hear more snoring. So soon again? You simply cannot believe it. Turning around, you see all three disciples fast asleep once again. Looking across the field to where the other eight disciples are lying on the ground, you can see that they are asleep, also. You wonder about the possible causes for their deep slumber, despite their effort to keep awake. Is it because of a heavy passover meal with wine at supper? Or is it because of the dark cloud of gloom that has descended over them due to the prophetic utterances of Jesus at the passover supper? Perhaps the latter is the cause.

According to the biblical account of the passover feast just before coming to the Garden of Gethsemane, Jesus prophesied to them about his impending death, that they all will forsake him, and that one of them will betray him. They have never seen Jesus this way before, so overcome with sorrow- so filled with gloom and doom. This sudden transfiguration of Jesus into a man of sorrow is a far cry, a disappointing disparity, from the transfiguration of Jesus on the mountain, as the Son of God in all his glory.

Indeed, they have seen Jesus turning water into wine, walking on water, calming the stormy sea, feeding five thousand people with five loaves and two fish, casting out devils, giving sight to the blind, healing the sick and raising the dead. This is the Messiah they have followed. They just cannot relate to the suffering Messiah.. The Messiah as a man of sorrow, and acquainted with grief is beyond their comprehension. Now fulfilling the prophesy of Isaiah, they "hid their faces" from the suffering Messiah. So, in the restful oblivion of sleep- in the weakness of the flesh- they hide themselves from the suffering Messiah. And soon all will forsake him. Every disciple will go into hiding when Judas the betrayer shows up with soldiers to arrest him, fulfilling the prophesy of Jesus.

Once again you hear footsteps approaching. You turn to see Jesus coming toward you. Walking over to where you are seated beside the three disciples, he sees them sleeping again. He then looks across the field to see the other eight disciples fast asleep as well. Jesus is all alone. No one to watch and pray with him. Nevertheless, the Lord's face is framed with a look of compassion as his eyes linger lovingly on the sleeping disciples. Without a word this time, he slowly turns around and heads back to his place of prayer.

There, beside the rock, Jesus remains praying for a long while. But now you can hardly hear him praying because of the heavy snoring of the disciples sleeping beside you. To say that soon every disciple will experience a rude awakening is an understatement. Indeed, it will be a traumatic awakening to terror, guilt and shame.

Judas Betrayal

From where you are sitting in the Garden of Gethsemane, you can see the Eastern wall of Jerusalem, the Kidron valley a short distance below Jerusalem, and also the foot hills of the Mount of Olives, just below the Garden of Gethsemane. Now your attention is drawn to lights moving rapidly up the foot hills of the Mount of Olives. A long string of lights is heading up the mountain side toward the Garden of Gethsemane. Multiple lights, looking like torch lights, are being carried by a small band of soldiers; you can see their armor gleaming in the light. Judging by their rate of speed, they should be here within minutes.

Now you see Jesus coming back the third time. Going over to Peter, James and John, he gently shakes them with the tenderness of a mother waking up a child. He says, "Sleep on now and take your rest. It is enough, the hour is come; behold the Son of Man is betrayed into the hands of sinners. Rise up, let us go; lo, he that betrayeth me is at hand."

The sound of the soldiers' feet can be heard, running now up the hill through the olive grove as they draw near to the Garden of Gethsemane. You hear the voice of their commanding officer urging them to run faster. Suddenly, you see a detachment of soldiers carrying flaming torches bursting in the grassy clearing of the Garden of Gethsemane. Standing with Jesus, Peter, James and John, you watch the soldiers moving toward the disciples on the other side of the field. By this time every disciple is wide awake. They are now huddled together, helpless like sheep attacked by ravenous wolves. The soldiers, in gleaming armor and with drawn swords, quickly surround them.

Then you see Judas, the betrayer. He is talking with the captain of the detachment from the chief priests while pointing in the direction where Jesus and the three disciples are standing. When Judas begins to move across the field toward Jesus, the captain barks an order for the soldiers to follow. As the soldiers quickly turn away from the disciples to follow Judas leading the way to Jesus, the disciples seize the opportunity to flee from the Garden of Gethsemane. You see them now desperately running across the field and then disappearing into the darkness of the surrounding olive grove. There is no effort on the part of the soldiers to stop them. Obviously their order is to arrest only Jesus. Their superiors know only too well that if you attack the shepherd, then the sheep will scatter.

Followed by the detachment of soldiers, Judas is now hurriedly walking across the field to where Jesus and the three disciples are standing. And as soon as he comes up to them, he goes straight to Jesus, saying, "Master! Master!" Then he kisses him.

Jesus says, "Judas, betrayest the Son of man with a kiss?"

The captain then nodded to two soldiers, who immediately seize Jesus, one grabbing his right hand the other his left.

Horrified at the ghastly sight of soldiers arresting Jesus, Peter suddenly pulls out a sword from under his garment, and lashes out wildly at one of the soldiers, cutting off his ear. But before Peter could strike again with the sword, the Lord stops him, saying sternly to him,

"Put up thy sword into its place, for all those who live by the sword shall die by the sword. Thinkest thou that I cannot now pray to my Father and he shall presently give me more than twelve legions of angels? But how then shall the scriptures be fulfilled, that thus it must be?"

The soldiers all seem awe struck by the power and authority that Jesus now exudes. The mention of his divine ability to summon angels seems to give them some pause in the act of arresting Jesus. Now, they seem indecisive and irresolute as they stand before him, looking quite awkward.

Jesus seems moved with compassion for the wounded soldier; his ear is bleeding profusely. Jesus says to him, "Suffer ye thus far." Then moving over to the wounded soldier, he touches his ear, and immediately his ear is healed and made whole again, the bleeding completely stanched.

The soldiers gasp in wonder and amazement. While the soldiers are preoccupied, focusing on the healing of the wounded soldier, Peter, James and John, quietly and quickly walk away, stealthily making their escape like the other disciples into the olive grove and disappearing into the darkness of the night.

Jesus is now left alone: All the disciples have left him and have fled, just as he prophesied at the passover supper that they would do. Like sheep they are now scattered.

Then Jesus turning to look at Judas, says, "Are ye come out as against a thief with swords and staves for to take me? I sat daily with you teaching in the temple, and ye laid no hold on me. But all this was done, that the scriptures of the prophets might be fulfilled."

Judas makes no response. He hangs his head down in shame. Indeed, the love of money is the root of all evil. Judas will deeply regret this night. But the hardness of his heart that led him to betray the Lord precludes the possibility of true repentance on his part. According to the biblical account of these events, Judas, unable to repent, will soon take his own life.

In Zechariah 11:12-13 the prophet Zechariah prophesied about the betrayal of Jesus by Judas. The prophet prophesied about the thirty silver coins that Judas would take as payment for betraying Christ. You are struck by this jolting realization: Jesus' worth is only thirty pieces of silver to Judas, but your worth to the Father is nothing less than the life of the Son of God. Jesus paid the penalty for sins by giving his life so that everyone who believes in him can live forever. But how terribly tragic that every unbeliever will suffer the fate of Judas. They will be judged and must pay the penalty for their own sins. Why? Because instead of responding to Jesus with a broken and contrite heart of repentance, they respond with a hardened heart to the amazing grace of God through Christ Jesus.

The Arrest of Jesus

It does not take long before the captain regains full control of the present situation. For the unbelieving mind, the witnessing of supernatural phenomena offer only a temporary distraction from their warped sense of duty. So once again you hear him barking orders to the soldiers. The same two soldiers again seize Jesus, pulling him along roughly as the detachment of soldiers begins to head back to Jerusalem.

In the moon light you follow the soldiers as they march rapidly behind the two soldiers who are hurriedly and brutally dragging Jesus. You follow them across the Garden of Gethsemane until you reach its far end. Then the soldiers, pulling Jesus along, turn down the path leading to the foot hills of the Mount of Olives. The specter of the shadow of Judas following, cast by the flickering light from the flaming torches, can be seen moving eerily down the hill behind the soldiers.

Although your view is partially obstructed by the trees in the olive grove, you can still see the lights from the torches that several soldiers are carrying. You watch them descending to the foot hills of the Mount of Olives and then crossing the Kidron Valley which separates the Mount of Olives from Jerusalem. Then in a little while you see the lights ascending from the valley to the Eastern wall of Jerusalem as the soldiers walk up the steep road leading to the eastern gate of the city. Entering the gate, the soldiers, with Jesus as their prisoner, disappear from your view.

The Curse of Sin is Lifted

You are now conscious of the deep silence around you. You turn around to view the empty garden, and you see a remarkable change. The wild flowers are no longer looking radiant and beautiful in the moon light, but their blossoms seem wilted and drooping. The lilies of the field that you observed before arrayed with such exquisite beauty are now seen crushed, and trampled on the ground by the marching feet of the soldiers. As you think about the unimaginable agony that the suffering Messiah, the holy One, is now going through, you just can't help but wondering if all creation– in heaven and on earth– is now groaning with a groaning that cannot be uttered.

But then this revelation dawns upon you: Creation is not groaning, but instead rejoicing. Why? The curse is lifted! The curse of sin is lifted from mankind. Tonight, when Jesus, in perfect obedience to the Father, chose to drink from the cup of suffering to pay the penalty of sin for mankind, when he travailed with the power of evil, sweating drops of blood, you saw then the beginning of the lifting of the curse of sin. Indeed, creation is rejoicing. All creation groaned until tonight, waiting for the redemption of mankind.

But tonight, the suffering Messiah, the new Adam in the garden of Gethsemane, in perfect obedience said YES to God: "Not my will, but thy will be done!" Creation is now rejoicing; redemption has come. Thank God, he lifted the curse that Adam in the garden of Eden caused, when in disobedience he said NO to God: "Not thy will, but my will be done!" The curse is lifted! Through the obedience of Christ, who paid the penalty for our sins, mankind can experience forgiveness of sin, and live a life of obedience to God.

Looking down on Jerusalem from the Mount of Olives, you now remember the biblical account of Jesus standing upon the Mount of Olives, and looking down on Jerusalem. Weeping over Jerusalem, for all its lost and condemned souls, Jesus said, " O Jerusalem, Jerusalem, thou that killest the prophets, and stonest them which are sent unto thee, how often would I have gathered thy children together, even as a hen gathereth her chickens under her wings, and ye would not."

Tomorrow the people of Jerusalem will put to death their Messiah– the Savior of the world. Why? Because as the Bible says, "The light shineth in darkness and the darkness comprehended it not." Indeed, the Jews in Jerusalem love darkness more than light, and so they will cry out tomorrow, "Crucify him, crucify him." And just why do they love darkness more than light? Again the Bible gives the answer. Because their deeds are evil. They live in disobedience, serving themselves instead of God. Therefore, Jesus wept over Jerusalem, because they chose darkness over the Light of the World; tomorrow they will choose Barrabas– a violent criminal– over Jesus, the Messiah.

Now you shudder, as you think about the coming events. Jesus will be taken to the chief priests to be interrogated and beatened, then to Pilate, then to Herod, then back to Pilate again. The Roman governor, Pilate, will be pressured by the unbelieving Jews to sentence him to death by crucifixion. Then there will be the awful scourging by the Romans, who will mercilessly beat him. Unimaginable torture now awaits Jesus! All because God so loved you, that he came to this sinful world to suffer for you and to die for you in order to pay the penalty for your sins. As you consider the awesome love of God, you find that at this moment you are loving God more than ever.

Thoughts about your timely visit with the faithful patriarch now enter your mind. You recall how God tested Abraham's love by commanding him to offer up his son, his only son Isaac as a sacrifice. Abraham passed the test of love, because like Jesus he did not say "no" to a commandment that seemed so shockingly dreadful and horrendous. Certainly Abraham's love for God and unwavering obedience to him is a foreshadow of the perfect love and perfect obedience of the Son to the Father. The Lord's love for the Father and obedience to him was demonstrated in his prayer to the Father, when he prayed, "Not my will, but thy will be done."

You suddenly thought about the rock which you saw Jesus kneeling beside while he was praying. The Bible says that he prayed with such agony that his sweat became drops of blood. Remembering that through the eyes of your imagination you saw the tears of Abraham on the rock where he prayed, you now wonder if there could be any tell-tale signs like that on the rock where Jesus just prayed. So, you walk back across the field of the garden of Gethsemane to the place where Jesus prayed, the rock with the cleft– a deep hole on one side.

And there you see it! The agony! His indescribable pain becoming liquified as drops of blood now gleams in the moon light on the smooth surface of the rock. You drop to your knees, then you fall upon the rock, and as you wrap your arms around it, you worship the Lamb of God. Now moved beyond measure with a heart overflowing with love and with tears of repentance coursing down your cheeks, you cried out to God, "Oh Lord, you paid with your precious blood a debt that you didn't owe, because I owed a debt that I couldn't pay! Thank you, thank you, thank you dear Lord!" And there on the blood stained rock, your tear drops mingle with his blood.

After praising and thanking God for his boundless love, with arms wrapped around the rock, you begin to feel a sweet release, a blessed feeling of a deep, settled peace. Then you stand up to take one last look on the garden of Gethsemane before leaving. You are alone now in the midst of the beautiful wild flowers, so conspicuously radiant in the moon light. You find the natural beauty of this place, nestled in the midst of olive trees, to be truly remarkable. You can certainly see why Jesus would take his disciples to a place like this. You can also understand the reason for Jesus taking his disciples so frequently to the Mount of Olives. According to the Bible, Jesus ascended to heaven from the Mount of Olives, and he will be returning to the earth on the Mount of Olives. Indeed, this mountain is a holy mountain.

And now you pray that the time you have spent here on this mountain in the holy presence of Jesus will be more than just a mental encounter. Indeed, the loving bond that you are now feeling for the Lord is an affirmation that this is a spiritual encounter. You truly believe that your timely visit with Jesus in the garden of Gethsemane will strengthened your spiritual relationship with the Lord, and enhance your love for God, who loves you more than you can ever imagine.

So realizing that it is time to take your leave from the Mount of Olives and to return to your time, you close the eyes of your imagination. And in the twinkling of an eye, traveling at the speed of thought, you find yourself back in your time– the present time.

Certainly your journey of the mind through time to visit Jesus was really a journey of the heart. The yearning of your heart to be nearer to God moved you to take this journey. And you know beyond the shadow of doubt that the Lord is well pleased with you now, because your heart has led you to obey his command to remember his great sacrifice for you. Could it be that you decided to take this journey when you heard his still small voice speaking to your heart to remember his great love for you? Of course, the answer is "Yes" to this question, if you truly feel spiritually blessed with the peace that passes all understanding, when you remember the amazing love of God.

Lessons Learned in Odyssey

The shedding of the blood of Jesus for the remission of sin started in the Garden of Gethsemane, when Jesus sweat drops of blood as he travailed in great agony while praying to the Father. The terrible agony that he felt in his soul when he travailed with the power of darkness was at least equal if not more than the physical pain he felt while nailed to the cross.

The last miracle of Jesus, the healing of his adversary's ear that was cut off by Peter, is remarkably different from other miracles. This miracle is unique in the sense that Jesus healed someone who opposed him.   As a servant of the high priest, who at the time was carrying out the diabolical bidding of his master, the soldier was an enemy of Christ. The might and power of Jesus that calmed the stormy sea, and raised the dead could crush in a moment the band of soldiers in the garden of Gethsemane. Instead, Jesus chose to heal the wounded soldier. This last miracle of healing by Jesus is a clear message for us to love our enemies, and to do good to our enemies.

Timely visit with Abraham on Mount Moriah: You are there

The following is taken from the biblical account of Abraham offering up his son, Isaac, as a sacrifice unto the Lord. (Genesis 22)

"And Abraham said, my son, God will provide himself a lamb for a burnt offering; so they went both of them together." (Genesis 22: 8)

Let the power of your imagination transport you once again to the time of Abraham, the great patriarch of Israel. If your mind is enlightened by the word and guided by the Holy Spirit, then your God- given imagination will be empowered to take you on another spiritual odyssey through time to the most crucial time in the life of Abraham.

This timely visit to the time of the great patriarch is a return visit to Abraham. You may remember that you were there with Abraham when the Lord commanded him to offer up his only son, Isaac, as a sacrifice. At that time you left the time of Abraham with the intention of making a second timely visit with Abraham on Mount Moriah . You left just as he was preparing to take Isaac and two servants with him to Mount Moriah, the place where he was commanded to offer up Isaac unto the Lord, as a burnt offering. So now get ready to return to see the subsequent unfolding events in the life of Abraham and Isaac. Hopefully you will also receive new insights about how these events are related to the plan of our redemption by God.

Just like you have done before, begin by reading the biblical account of Abraham offering up his son as a sacrifice unto the Lord, and prayerfully meditate upon your reading. Then open the eyes of your imagination, focusing your mind on Abraham, Isaac, the two servants, and also focusing on the land of Moriah, about three days journey from Abraham's home that you previously visited. And again, with the speed of thought, in the twinkling of an eye, you are traveling through time, far back to the past to arrive in the year 1872 BC. Looking around you seem to be standing above a naked wilderness.

The Center of the Earth

You have arrived on top of Mount Moriah, the place where Abraham is commanded by God to offer up Isaac, his only son, as a burnt offering. Looking around you can see that the surrounding land of Moriah is a far cry from what it will look like when it becomes the bustling city of Jerusalem in the time of Christ about 1900 years in the future. There are no tall, massive gray stone walls, no gold embellished temple, no white marble villas, and no houses, roads, or people to be seen anywhere. The land of Moriah at this time is a naked wilderness– uncultivated, uninhabited; it is an inhospitable looking region. Yet this place is ordained by God to be the center of the earth, the most holy city, where the glory of God some day will come down to dwell in the holy temple that Solomon will build at a future time.

Across from mount Moriah to the East is the mountain that will be called the Mount of Olives in the time of Christ. It is only about two miles away. But now looking through the eyes of your imagination, there are no olive trees on the mountain, only a thick vegetation and trees indigenous to the region. Close to the base of the mountain you see a grassy clearing in the midst of the thick vegetation covering the side of the mountain. You immediately identify this grassy patch on the mountain to be the location of the garden of Gethsemane, the site that you visited on your last timely visit.

But you are amazed that this grassy clearing on the mountain exists even at this time period. Why is this location, which will become the exact location of the Garden of Gethsemane over 1900 years from now, not overgrown with vegetation like the rest of the mountain? Is it set apart as the place where the Seed of Abraham, Jesus, the

Messiah, will choose to do the will of the Father by drinking from the cup of suffering? Also, is it possible that no vegetation can grow there because it is being preserved to become the field of blood, where Jesus suffered such agony of the soul that he sweat drops of blood? Indeed, such questions pertaining to the future location of the Garden of Gethsemane on the mountain can certainly be asked. But you realize that any answer to these questions would be purely speculative, because you are viewing the land of Moriah through the eyes of your imagination. Yet in this wonderland of the mind you can't help but wonder about such possible scenarios.

As you view the mountain that in time will be called the Mount of Olives, you are reminded of the teaching of the Bible that from this mountain Jesus will ascend into heaven, and this is also where he will descend upon his return from heaven. Indeed, no wonder this place is called the center of the earth; it is the gateway to and from heaven.

Turning to look North East from Mount Moriah, you see a hill that is shaped like a skull. It is less than a quarter mile away. In the time of Jesus this hill will be called Mount Calvary or Golgotha, meaning in Hebrew, the place of the skull. It is on this hill, in the shape of a skull, that the Lord will be crucified as the Lamb of God. There on Mount Calvary, within sight of Mount Moriah, Jesus will be sacrificed for the sins of the world.

Here as you stand on Mount Moriah, the genesis of God's plan to redeem the human race comes into focus. You can see with stunning clarity how the offering up of Isaac as a sacrifice is a foreshadow of the Son of God to be sent to this world by the Father as a sacrifice for the sins of the human race: "For God so loved the world that he gave his only begotten Son that whosoever believes on him should not perish, but have everlasting life." This is the place, Mount Moriah, where the plan of redemption will begin, and over there on Mount Calvary, about nineteen hundred years from now, it will be completed, when Jesus shall declare, "It is finished." Indeed, this holy land is truly the center of the earth.

Isaac as a Type of Christ

Looking down into the Kidron Valley to the South you can see the distant forms of figures far away, moving toward the land of Moriah. No doubt it is Abraham coming with Isaac, his two servants, and with his donkey, carrying the wood for the burnt offering. In your excitement to see them, you immediately scamper down the side of Mount Moriah, hurriedly make your way down to the Kidron Valley, and then turning South, you continue on your way to meet them.

While walking rapidly toward them, you notice how slowly they are moving up the hill. As you draw near to them, you can see how tired and weary everyone is. Of course, they would be tired and weary now, after the three days journey to the land of Moriah. Abraham, Isaac and the two servants are all dragging their feet with the weariness of their journey. They are all covered with the dust and grime of their long journey, and sweating profusely in the heat of the day. The donkey is also walking wearily under the load of wood on his back. But you are simply amazed that despite Abraham's old age– well over a hundred years– he is still able to take such an arduous journey.

Just as you reach to within a few feet of them, Abraham, who is walking in front, raises his hand as a signal for everyone to stop. He is steadfastly looking in your direction. And at that moment this amusing thought comes to your mine: "Looks like they are stopping for me. But I'm here only mentally not physically." As they stop to wait for Abraham to speak, your attention is drawn to Isaac, Abraham's son. You are surprised to see how much his physical appearance is like the biblical description of David; the shepherd boy, whom God someday will anoint king over Israel by the prophet Samuel. David, living about 800 years after the time of Abraham is described in the Bible to be "ruddy, and with a beautiful countenance, and goodly to look on." Certainly, the fourteen year old boy, standing before you now, fits that description.

Abraham, looking toward Mount Moriah, says to his two servants, "Abide you here with the ass, and I and the lad will go yonder and worship, and come again unto you."

Standing there watching the two servants taking the load of wood for the burnt offering from the back of the donkey, and placing it on the shoulder of Isaac, you remember the biblical account describing how the cross was laid on the shoulder of Christ. Certainly this incredible event that you are now watching is a shadow of the most incredible event that is yet to come: The sacrifice of Christ, the Son of God. Indeed, this event is a foreshadow of God's plan to give his Son as a ransom for sin- the sacrifice of Jesus as the Lamb of God. The reason why Isaac is considered to be a type of Christ by all Christian theologians is now becoming abundantly clear to you.

Entering Holy Ground

Abraham directs his servant to light the torch that is strapped on the servant's back. You watch with fascination as the servant starts a fire to light the torch. Of course, matches to light a fire is nonexistent in the time of Abraham, so the servant uses the most common method to light a fire at that time. Kneeling on the ground, the servant places a thin wooden shaft within a notch against the soft wooden base of a fire board, and begins to spin the shaft rapidly creating a glowing coal from the wood dust. The hot coal is then placed on the torch. And voila! The fire is ignited on the torch. The fire from the torch is to be used to set on fire the burnt offering– Abraham's son, Isaac. The servant now gives the flaming torch to Abraham

Taking the flaming torch, Abraham now directs the servant to give him the long knife that is tucked under a belt around his waist. After the bundle of wood is securely balanced on the shoulder of Isaac, Abraham gestures to Isaac, carrying the bundle of wood, to start walking up the hill to Mount Moriah. Isaac obeys his father and begins to climb the hill leading up to the mountain. Holding the flaming torch in one hand and the knife in the other, Abraham follows Isaac up the steep hill side.

As you follow Abraham and Isaac up the hill, you begin to wonder about Abraham's motives for leaving his two servants and the donkey behind. Of course there is the obvious motive: It is a preemptive measure. He would not want his servants there with him while killing Isaac, because, no doubt, they would stop their master from murdering his own son. But there has to be another motive. You can understand the obvious motive for leaving his servants behind, but why did he also leave the donkey behind? Surely, he could have used the donkey to carry the load of wood to the holy site of the burnt offering.

Suddenly, you are struck by this thought: It's now a holy place!

Now you can see clearly that Abraham's real motive, no doubt, would be to keep Mount Moriah from being defiled by his servants. It is holy ground. The holy presence of God is there. Abraham couldn't take anyone or anything to that holy place. You are also struck by the thought that in the garden of Gethsemane, Jesus also left his three disciples behind in order to go to a place set apart– a holy place, and to spend time alone with the Father– a holy time with his Father. In the same way Isaac is now alone with his father, Abraham. And soon father and son will enter the holy presence of God.

Your thoughts turn to the holy of holies in the temple in Jerusalem during the time of Christ. Many centuries from now, the temple will be built on Mount Moriah, and doubtlessly the holy of holies in the temple will occupy the exact site of the altar where Abraham will offer up today his burnt offering unto the Lord. Because this is such a holy ground, only the High Priest of the temple will be allowed to enter the holy of holies– that is until the time when Jesus paid the penalty for sins on the cross.

When Jesus died for your sins, the Bible says that the veil of the temple was torn apart, allowing believers to access the holy of holies– the presence of God. Because of the blood of Jesus that cleanses you from all your sins, you can now enter the holy of holies to be in the presence of your heavenly Father.

While following the two patriarchs up the hill to Mount Moriah, you are beginning to feel a deep reverence for the holiness of God. Also, you are feeling profound gratitude that as a believer in Christ, who is cleansed from all your sin, you can enter at any time the holy of holies– the holy presence of Abba, your heavenly Father. Whenever you pray in the name of Jesus, you enter the presence of God.

Walking the Via Dolorosa– The Way of Sorrow

As you watch through the eyes of your imagination Isaac going up through the Kidron valley then turning up a steep hill toward Mount Moriah, while struggling with the heavy load of wood on his shoulder, you are moved with compassion for him. Indeed, he is still just a mere child. Of course, Abraham with his advanced age, is unable to help him. It seems that he can barely carry his own weight up the hill. Also his hands are not free; one hand is holding a torch, and the other, a knife. Suddenly, Isaac slides backward, his right foot slipping over loose soil on the steep hillside. But he manages to remain erect, steadying the bundle of wood on his shoulder.

As you watch Isaac straining to carry the heavy load, you wish you could really be here physically instead of just mentally. How you would like to help him carry the bundle of wood to Mount Moriah, like how the Bible describes Simeon, helping to carry the cross of Jesus to Mount Calvary. The obvious comparison of Isaac struggling to carry his bundle of wood with Jesus struggling to carry his cross, both on their way to be sacrificed, now comes to your mind.

Your thoughts now turn to Jesus, walking on the Via Dolorosa– the road of sorrow. In the time of Christ, the Via Dolorosa will pass by the temple that will be built on Mount Moriah, then it will pass through the city of Jerusalem, which is the land of Moriah, and finally the Via Dolorosa will end at the place of the skull, Mount Calvary, also called Golgotha. After being beaten to within an inch of his life, the man of sorrow, will walk the long and winding road of sorrow, so that someday all our tears of sorrow can be wiped away. Oh what sacrifice of love! Truly, God is love!

As Isaac is walking up the hill toward Mount Moriah, you look to the right to see the hill shaped like a skull, which will be called Mount Calvary in the time of Christ. And the thought enters your mind: Someday the path of Jesus– the Via Dolorosa– will cross the path that Isaac is now taking, carrying the bundle of wood, on his way to be offered up as a burnt offering for a sacrifice unto the Lord. Indeed, centuries from now, on the way to Mount Calvary, Jesus will cross Isaac's path carrying his cross to be sacrificed for the sins of the world. How truly amazing that God has ordained Isaac to be such a type of Christ– pointing us to Jesus as the "Lamb that takes away all our sins."

The Lord will provide

Out of breath and straining with all his might to carry the heavy load of wood up the steep mountain side, Isaac, with a prodigious effort, finally manages to reach near to the top of Mount Moriah. Then you hear him calling out to Abraham, "My father!"

Abraham answers, "Here am I"

Sweating profusely and breathing heavily, he says, "Behold the wood and the fire, but where is the lamb for a burnt offering?"

Looking up toward heaven, Abraham says, "My son, God will provide himself a lamb for a burnt offering."

Through the eyes of your imagination, you also look up toward heaven. There is blue sky everywhere, except over Mount Moriah. Now you see that there is a white shining cloud hovering above the mountain. The cloud that is hovering above is the exact same size as the area on the top of the mountain.

As you gaze upon the white cloud gleaming in the noon day sun with a bright shining silver lining around its contour, the still small voice of the Spirit speaks to your heart these words of Psalm 104:3, "God lays the beams of his chambers in the waters, he makes the clouds his chariot, and he walks upon the wings of the winds." Assuredly, God is here! And how can one say that God is here? Because faith is here. Indeed, Abraham believes that God will provide. And where there is faith, there is God.

Abraham and Isaac continue climbing up the steep side of the mountain, until finally they reach the top of Mount Moriah. Exhausted beyond measure, so tired and so weary, after carrying such a heavy load up the steep hill, Isaac can't wait to get rid of the heavy load. Immediately, he casts down his heavy burden, the pieces of wood tumbling down upon the ground. As soon as Abraham sets his feet upon Mount Moriah, he lifts up his head and hands toward heaven. He sees the cloud. He gazes with deep reverence upon the bright shining cloud, hovering above so close to the top of Mount Moriah. Isaac, looking up also, gazes upon the cloud that has descended so near to the mountain. Then Abraham moves into action; He begins to build an altar for the burnt offering. At this point, the Bible gives no details about his action in building the altar, but leaves that to your imagination. So, what do you see?

Abraham places the flaming torch between two rocks, wedging it against the rocks to keep it upright. He also places the knife on one of the rocks. So now, his hands are free to build the altar. Both Abraham and Isaac begin to pick up rocks seen everywhere on Mount Moriah. They carry these rocks to the place where they first set their feet on the mountain. Abraham with the help of Isaac now begins the building of the altar, by carefully placing the rocks upon each other in a pile large enough to accommodate the burnt offering. Then they lay the pieces of wood Isaac carried, upon the altar. Finally, their task is completed; the altar is now ready for the burnt offering. No doubt, Isaac is still wondering: Where is the lamb for the burnt offering?

At this point the Bible gives few details about Isaac's reaction with the realization that he was the burnt offering. So, you can only speculate about Isaac's response. So, what do you see when you look through the eyes of imagination?

Reaching under his garment, Abraham pulls out a rope, and holding Isaac's hands together, he wraps the rope around his hands, tying the rope tightly, binding his son's hands. Totally caught off guard by this unexpected action, Isaac does not know what to think. Is it a joke? Puzzled, and appearing confused, he searches his father's face for an answer. At once, he realizes that this is not a joke. There is a mournful look on Abraham's face, tears of grief are coursing down his cheeks, saturating his beard.

Isaac now terrified, asks the same question he asked before, but this time with a stammering tongue, "My father, behold the wood and the fire, but where is the lamb for a burnt offering?"

And Abraham gives the same answer as before, "My son, God will provide himself a lamb for the burnt offering."

You marvel at Abraham's faith. He still believes that God will provide a way. No doubt, he believes that even if Isaac is killed today, then God will raise him up. Abraham's faith is so strong because he truly knows the heart of God. He knows that God is too good to be unkind, and God is too wise to be mistaken. And he knows the love of God, and that he is at the center of God's heart.

And now you marvel at your lack of faith, because you are also at the center of God's heart. And yet how often your faith is marred with doubts.

Then bending down to kneel before his son, Abraham ties his feet, also. Standing there beside the altar, Isaac seems frozen with sudden terror. There is a horrified look on his face. His hands and feet bound, resistance is futile. Holding Isaac around his waist, Abraham pulls him gently toward the altar. Then lifting up his son he places him on the pieces of wood on the altar of sacrifice. His face is washed with tears. No doubt, right now Abraham wishes that he could change place with his son. But that cannot be.

Isaac cries out to Abraham, "My father, my father why are you doing this to me.?"

Abraham answers, "My son, the Lord whom we both love and serve, has commanded me to do this. The Lord said to me, 'Take now thy son, thine only son, Isaac, whom thou lovest, and get thee into the land of Moriah, and offer him there for a burnt offering upon one of the mountains which I will tell thee of.'"

Stupefied and shock beyond measure, Isaac asks in a weak, tremulous voice, "Why? Why? Why?

Looking down tenderly on his son, Abraham answers, "My son, know in your heart that the Lord truly loves you. And I love you. Trust in the Lord. He will provide."

As you stand there, looking down on Isaac, with his hands and feet bound, lying on the wood upon the altar, your thoughts turn to Jesus hanging on the cross, his hands and feet nailed to the cross. And from the bottom of your heart you thank God for providing his Lamb who died and paid the penalty for your sins. And not only for your sin, but for Isaac's sin, Abraham's sin and for the sin of all who trust in Jesus as the Lamb of God, whom God has provided, because he so loved us. Indeed, the words that you now hear spoken by Abraham are prophetic: "The Lord will provide for himself a lamb." In the fullness of time God will provide the Lamb of God.

Abraham walks over to fetch the knife that he left on the rock close by. Returning to the altar he now holds down Isaac on the altar with his left hand. Isaac is seized with terror. But as Abraham is raising his right hand to plunge the knife in the heart of his son, suddenly a voice, sounding like rolling thunder, is heard from heaven.

From the cloud above, the angel of the Lord calls, "Abraham! Abraham!"

Looking up at the cloud, Abraham answers, "Here am I."

Isaac, also hearing the voice from heaven, raises up to look on the bright shining cloud above.

In a voice of thunder, the Lord says, "Lay not thine hand upon the lad, neither do thou anything unto him, for now I know that thou fearest God, seeing that thou hast not withheld thy son, thine only son from me."

The answer to his prayer! Hearing such gracious words from the Lord, Abraham bursts out with a loud cry of sheer joy. He envelops his son in a crushing bear hug, then quickly unties the bonds around his hands and feet. Getting up from the altar, Isaac hugs his father, his face now framed with exquisite ecstasy.

The rolling thunder of the voice from heaven is again heard, as the angel of the Lord calls from the cloud, saying to Abraham, "By myself have I sworn, saith the Lord, for because thou hast done this thing, and has not withheld thy son, thine only son, that in blessing I will bless thee and in multiplying I will multiply thy seed as the stars of the heaven and as the sand which is upon the sea shore, and thy seed shall possess the gate of his enemies. And in thy seed shall all the nations of the earth be blessed, because thou hast obey my voice."

As you listen to these prophetic words of the Lord, you marvel at the divine plan of redemption of mankind. You can see so clearly now that God in his great wisdom commanded Abraham to sacrifice his son as the means to initiate his wonderful plan of redemption. God's command for a loving father to offer up his only son as a sacrifice was only a dry run for the time when the heavenly Father would offer up his Son, his only begotten Son as the Lamb of God. In the fulfillment of time God would send Christ Jesus, the Son of God, to die on the cross as a sacrifice for the sins of the world. The Lord's promise to Abraham that "in thy seed shall all the nations of the earth be blessed, because thou hast obey my voice" is fulfilled in Jesus– the Seed of Abraham. All the nations would be blessed, due to the death, burial and resurrection of Israel's Messiah. Indeed, Jesus has brought the greatest blessing to the world by redeeming people of all nations from the curse of sin.

Suddenly, Abraham hears a rustling sound in the thicket behind him. Turning around to look, he sees a ram caught by his horn in the dense growth of bushes. The ram is trapped in the thicket in such a way that he is completely unable to extricate himself from the bushes. Indeed, Abraham's prayer has been answered: The Lord has provided himself a lamb. Truly God is the great provider. And great is his faithfulness. Suddenly, the praise of God gushes from the depths of your soul, and you hear yourself shouting, "Hallelujah! Hallelujah! Hallelujah! Praise God forevermore!"

Looking with the eyes of imagination on the white ram with the long horn, you begin to wonder how the ram got to Mount Moriah. Could this be the same ram that you saw before on your previous timely visit to Abraham's home? Was this ram sent from Beer-Sheba to Mount Moriah for such a time as this? But of course, you recognize these questions to be quite speculative, based not on the Word but based on your imagination. However, these questions are only food for thought when one considers the realm of possibilities concerning the ram coming to Mount Moriah. Indeed, it is essential to be circumspect and to see everything in the right perspective. Therefore, in the final analysis, how God does something is far less important than what he does. The Bible reveals the marvelous acts of God.

According to the biblical account of this event, you know that soon Abraham will extract the ram from the thicket, and offer him up for a burnt offering in the place of his son, Isaac. But now through the eye of imagination, you see Abraham and Isaac kneeling down before the altar. It appears that they are both offering up a prayer of thanksgiving unto the Lord.

Again, you turn to look on the ram, caught in the thicket. He seems to be experiencing some pain or agony as he vainly struggles to get out. You hear the sound of his bleating- a wavering cry that sounds so pitiful. And you remember the agony of Jesus in the garden of Gethsemane. His pain was so intense that his sweat became drops of blood. You look down at the location that will be called the garden of Gethsemane several hundred years from now. Suddenly, you are feeling the urge to walk down to the garden. Glancing back at

Abraham and Isaac, you see that they are still praying. You decide to leave them now while they are praying.

The Rock of Ages

Walking down from Mount Moriah you head straight down to the Kidron Valley, then in a few minutes, after crossing the valley, you begin to ascend the mountain. You veer to the left as you move up the mountain to the grassy clearing, where Jesus, hundreds of years from now, will spend his last night before his crucifixion. In about twenty minutes you arrive at the location that will be called the Garden of Gethsemane, situated at the foot of the mountain to be called at a future time, the Mount of Olives.

And the sight before your eyes is utterly unbelievable. Nothing has changed! The garden is just the same as your last timely visit about 1900 years in the future from the time of Abraham. Again you see the same beautiful wild flowers, and the same rocks in the garden as before. The size and shape of the garden remain the same. To be sure, your timely visit at the time of Christ was at night, but it was a bright moon lit night and so you could see everything in the garden. Suddenly, you remember how you saw through the eye of imagination the rock where Jesus prayed while leaning upon it- the rock on which his sweat could be seen as drops of blood.

You walk over to the far side of the garden, where you remember the rock to be. And there you see it; the same rock with the unique appearance- oval in shape with a deep cleft, a hole in its side. You fall to your knees beside the rock, and wrap your arms around it, hugging it close to you. You remember the time before, when you saw through the eye of imagination the tell-tale signs of the Lord's agony upon this rock- his sweat becoming drops of blood; his blood that was shed for you. Oh the precious blood of Jesus!

While kneeling there, with arms wrapped around the rock, the words of this song comes to your mind:

"Rock of ages, cleft for me

Let me hide myself in thee

Let the water and the blood

From thy wounded side which flowed

Be of sin the double cure

Save from wrath and make me pure."

Indeed, Jesus is the blessed rock, the living rock. He is the solid rock that is unmovable, and unshakable– the unchanging God that is the same, yesterday, today and forever. Kneeling before the rock, you pray for a long while. And there you remain for a good while longer, glorifying and worshiping the Lord.

Then remembering that Abraham and Isaac are still on Mount Moriah, you turn to look toward the mountain. And you see a column of smoke rising from the top of Mount Moriah to the bright shining cloud above. Evidently, Abraham has sacrificed the ram that the Lord provided. As you watch the smoke of the burnt offering rising up to the Lord, you know that the Lord is receiving the burnt offering as a sweet smelling incense, because it is seasoned with the love and obedience of Abraham. And now there is a burning desire in your heart to have the same love and obedience for the Lord; to be hidden in the cleft of the rock like Abraham.

Then through the eye of imagination, you see a most wonderful sight. The bright shining cloud above Mount Moriah is rapidly changing, morphing into the shape of a giant cross. Then the cross begins to rise higher and higher. The cross of Christ can be seen now standing high in the air above Mount Moriah. How marvelous, how wonderous to see! Indeed, Mount Moriah is a foreshadow of Mount Calvary; it now stands under the shadow of the cross. You gaze upon the shining white cloud shaped like a cross for a long while until finally the cloud disperses in the gentle wind that is now softly caressing your face.

Soon you see Abraham and Isaac coming from Mount Moriah heading down toward the Kidron Valley. Reaching the valley they turn in the direction where they left the two servants waiting with the donkey. You can still see them in the distance, when they reach the place where the servants are standing beside the donkey. Then you see Abraham, hugging his son, Isaac, and helping him up to sit on the donkey. They now turn around to go back the way they came. After seeing Isaac earlier, carrying such a heavy load of wood up to Mount Moriah, you are glad to see that he is now riding the donkey. They now begin the three day journey that will take them back home to Beer-Sheba.

As you watch Abraham taking his leave from the land of Moriah, you realize that it is time to take your leave, also. Certainly it was good for you to be here. Again you feel that this journey back in time is much more than a mental journey. Indeed, it was a spiritual journey. Here and now, you are still feeling the presence of the Lord. And you pray that his sweet, comforting presence will rest and abide with you. So now you close the eye of your imagination and in a moment, in a twinkling of an eye, you are back to the present.

Lessons Learned in Odyssey

Isaac, who was offered up to God by his father, Abraham, as a burnt offering or sacrifice, is a type of Christ. The willingness of Abraham to sacrifice his son is a foreshadow of God, the Father, sending the Son of God, Christ Jesus, to die on the cross as a sacrifice for our sins. But only Christ Jesus, who is God in the flesh, could be the ultimate sacrifice for sin. Jesus paid the penalty of sin in full on the cross.

The promise that God made to Abraham that from his "seed" all nations of the earth would be blessed was fulfilled in the coming of Israel's Messiah, Jesus. All nations have been blessed through Christ. God has chosen people from all nations of the earth to be his children through their faith in Jesus as Savior and Lord. As born again children of God, born of the Spirit, they are blessed with the greatest blessing– everlasting life.

Timely Visit with Moses: You Are There

The following is based on the account of the life of Moses, recorded in Exodus 3 and 4.

"I will now turn aside and see this great sight, why the bush is not burnt." (Exodus 3:3)

Although it might not be possible for you to physically travel through time, nevertheless, God has given you a special gift- your mind- that can become a mental time machine to transport you back to the past. You have already experienced the efficacy of this special gift, when mentally you were transported to the past to the time of Abraham and to the time of Jesus. In the same way, you can now also make a timely visit to the time of Moses, to see the sign and wonder of the burning bush. Of course, you must first be guided by the divine GPS, the word of God. If your mind is truly guided by the word of God, it is possible that the Holy Spirit will give you new insights and new revelations about this amazing event taking place, at the time just before the birth of the nation of Israel.

To visit the burning bush somewhere on Mount Horeb, and sometime in the distant past, about 1500 BC, enter now the time machine of your mind. Because the speed of thought is even faster than the speed of light, your mind, which is empowered by the imagination, will take you instantly to your destination. So get ready for your timely visit; focus on the event of the burning bush, taking place now somewhere far, far away and sometime long, long ago. Imagine the place, Mount Horeb, and the time, 1500 BC. Here you are now! Open the eyes of your imagination to see what you can see.

Tongues of Fire

The sight above you is incredibly beautiful. You see clouds above the far horizon and clouds high above the vast grassy plain where you are standing. The clouds are ablaze with shining colors of fiery red and flaming yellow, and with exquisite shades of shimmering purple, and glowing radiantly with the color of incandescent amber. The unusual formation of the clouds with flaming colors look like tongues of fire. Your eyes are filled with the radiant beauty of the most glorious sunset. The heavenly view literally takes your breath away; you gasp with wonder at the incredibly beautiful heavenly sight.

You now turn around to see, looming before you and reaching toward heaven, a mountainous and humongous wilderness of rocks; awesome in appearance is the massive mountain of God, Mount Horeb, also called Mount Sinai. The granite crags of the mountain rise high, towering upward. It is so incredibly high that you are experiencing some dizziness as you tilt your head backward to view the top of the mountain. High above the mountain, you see another pillar of fiery red cloud.

You stand there for a while, gazing at the awesome sight looming before you. Glancing away from the top of Mount Horeb, suddenly you see on one of the mountain slopes flames of fire engulfing a clump of bush. The burning bush! The sight of the burning bush– the sign of the holy presence of God– fills you with a deep sense of awe and adoration. The burning bush is located on one of the slopes of the mountain, thick with vegetation; it seems to be only a few hundred feet above the base of Mount Horeb.

You begin now to run with mounting excitement across the grassy plain toward the mountain. Reaching the base of the mountain, you climb up the steep mountainside. You hurriedly make your way over large boulders of rock, your heart beating faster with excitement as you get closer to the burning bush. Reaching within a couple hundred feet of the burning bush, you can see clearly the leaping flames of fire directly above you on the slope of the mountain. Then climbing up the steep side of the mountain to the edge of the slope, you pull yourself over its edge until finally you are standing on the slope where you can get a close up view of the burning bush. While moving toward the bush with flames of fire gushing from it, you suddenly remember: this is holy ground. You stop abruptly, not daring to go further. With your eyes still fixed on the burning bush, you seat yourself on one of the large boulders nearby. Sitting there, you watch with hypnotic fascination the bush completely inundated with flames of fire.

You stare with wonder and amazement on the incredible sight of a bush engulfed with the flames of fire without being consumed. Not even a single leaf or the smallest twig on the bush appears to be singed by the flames of the fire. From where you are seated, you can feel the heat of the fire. Although the flames are gushing from inside the bush, surprisingly, it still remains vibrantly green and lush in its appearance. There is no crackling sound from the fire; the gushing flames are completely noiseless. And there is no smoke. It seems that the fire engulfing the bush is having the same effect as a shower of rain would have falling upon it. The burning bush seems completely untouched by the devouring flames. The leaves of the bush are animated with movement while the tongues of fire are ceaselessly licking at them; You watch the leaves dance in the fire like leaves dancing in the wind.

Then an incredible insight suddenly comes to you as you recall a well-known Bible verse in Acts 2:38: "And tongues of fire sat upon each of them." For the first time, you are beginning to see an amazing connection between the phenomenon of the burning bush and the supernatural phenomenon of the Holy Spirit on the Day of Pentecost. On the Day of Pentecost, the disciples received the Holy Spirit from heaven while they tarried in the upper room at Jerusalem. They also saw at that time and in that place flames of fire upon each of them, but the fire did not consume them.

According to the Bible, "tongues of fire sat upon each of them," and like the burning bush, they were not burned nor consumed by the fire. Like Moses at the burning bush on this mountain, they too experienced the awesome presence of the Lord at the upper room in Jerusalem. The sudden awareness that on this mental journey you are beginning to see the spiritual realm with greater clarity fills you with a sense of wonder. You wonder if this could be a sign that your mental journey is becoming a spiritual journey.

The extraordinary connection between the events of the upper room and the burning bush is absolutely stunning as you continue to see other comparisons between the two events. Suddenly, you are experiencing an unexpected moment of clarity. It is becoming wondrously clear to you that Mount Horeb relates to Moses' ministry, as the upper room on the Day of Pentecost relates to the disciples's ministry. The disciples and Moses, after their encounter with God, were empowered to do great miracles; indeed, this appears to be the time and place where Moses, like the disciples, will be baptized with the Holy Spirit, which will empower him to do great miracles.

These words of the Bible reverberate through your mind: "They will be baptized with the Holy Ghost and fire." It seems to you that Moses' encounter with the burning bush– the Spirit of God in the midst of the fire speaking to Moses– represents the baptism of Moses with the Holy Ghost and fire. Here and now, you will get to see Moses as he is baptized with the Holy Spirit at the burning bush upon Mount Horeb. He will never be the same again. In the same way, the disciples were baptized with the Holy Spirit, as tongues of fire came upon them at the upper room. Also, they were never the same again. Indeed, from now on, the power of the Holy Spirit in Moses will become "like a fire shut up in his bones."

Weary, Weak, and Worn

Before the burning bush, you now sit waiting with mounting excitement to see Moses, while a stream of thought about this great man of God fills your mind. Hebrew by birth, he became prince of Egypt, when he was adopted by Pharaoh's daughter. However, he was exiled from Egypt when Pharaoh found out that he killed an Egyptian who was abusing a Hebrew. Today you will witness at this burning bush Moses' great calling by God: Israel's greatest leader and lawgiver.

And now you hear the sound of the bleating of sheep. Looking down the side of the mountain to the grassy plain below, where you were standing before, you see a large flock of sheep. They are heading in a direction that is taking them away from the mountain. A shepherd is seen walking at some distance behind the sheep; he seems to be dragging his tall, lanky frame along with some difficulty. He appears to be weary, weak, and worn. He is using his long shepherd's staff as a walking stick while he shuffles wearily along behind the sheep. Moses!

You feel the impulse to call to him. But this sight is so incongruous to your image of Moses that you wonder if your imagination is still under your control or again guided by an "autopilot;" you have never imagined him to look like this. Certainly, he does not look to you now like a prince, or any kind of a leader, for that matter.

He stops for a moment and turns around to gaze upon the beautiful sunset. He stands there, his eyes drinking in the glorious sunset with its shining colors of fiery red and flaming orange with stunning shades of amber and purple. As he stands there, gazing on the sunset, you can see his face plainly. Despite his long flowing white beard and his hair appearing white as snow, he has a strikingly youthful-looking face, which belies his venerable age. According to the Bible, at this time in his life, Moses is about eighty years old.

There is something about his eyes, the expression on his face and his demeanor that arrest your attention. There seems to be a yearning, the appearance of pent-up feelings, a searching kind of expression on his face as he gazes on the sunset–like someone searching for a sign. His shoulders heave with a deep sigh. He then turns away, almost reluctantly, and continues to hobble along behind the sheep with his shepherd staff supporting him– weak, weary, and worn.

While he is walking away from the mountain, you wonder how will he see the burning bush and be drawn to the mountain of God. But he stops once again to turn and to gaze for a second time upon the glorious sunset. Lifting his head to look high above, he sees the fire in the sky– the pillar of red cloud, glowing in the setting sun like flames of fire. As he is looking up, out of the corner of his eyes, he glimpses the light of the fire on the mountain. Turning around, he sees the burning bush.

With a puzzled and curious expression on his face, Moses mutters out loud to himself a few words that you do not understand. This is not surprising to you; his language would obviously be Hebrew, the language spoken by the Israelites. However, due to your knowledge of the translation of these words in the Bible, you know that he is now saying, "I will now turn aside and see this great sight, why the bush is not burnt." Fixing his eyes on the burning bush, he drags his tall, lanky, weary-looking frame across the grassy plain, supported by his long shepherd's staff, and then climbs up the steep mountainside to finally reach the narrow rocky slope where the burning bush is situated.

He walks by you, where you are seated on the rock, his face framed with a look of bewilderment. Staring intently on the bush engulfed with flames, he slowly and cautiously makes his approach, then stops a few feet away from the burning bush. For several minutes he stands there dumbfounded, watching the green leaves in the flames dancing, animated by the tongues of fire.

Holy Ground

The puzzled and curious expression that was on his face at his first sight of the burning bush has now changed to an expression of wonder and amazement. As he starts to move closer to examine the flaming bush, suddenly a loud voice, rumbling like the sound of rolling thunder, calls out from inside the bush. "Moses! Moses! "Startled by the unexpected thunderous voice, Moses falls down, but somehow manages to break his fall by frantically using his shepherd's staff to keep from falling to the ground. After a long moment, while his trembling hands gripped tightly his staff, in a quivering voice and with a stammering tongue, he answers, "Here am I."

The voice booms from inside the burning bush, "Draw not nigh hither; put off thy shoes from off thy feet, for the place where on thou stand is holy ground."

With one hand still gripping his staff, Moses, with his other hand, hurriedly removes his shoes. Using the staff to pull himself up in a more erect position, he kneels before the burning bush. He kneels there, trembling while he looks steadfastly on the fire, his eyes bulging wide in fright and his face ashen and taut. Moses now seems riveted where he kneels– overcome with the awful fear of the unknown.

The voice, like a clap of thunder, roars again. "I am the God of thy father, the God of Abraham, the God of Isaac, and the God of Jacob."

It seems that the realization that he is before Almighty God, the creator of the universe and the creator of life, utterly blows his mind. His fear of the unknown is now dwarfed by the awful fear of divine judgment as he faces the holy, the all-knowing, and the all-powerful God, infinite and eternal. So Moses hides his face with one hand, afraid to look in the direction of God; perhaps believing that his guilt-ridden soul is about to be consumed by the holy God, who is like a consuming fire.

The God of Love

However, while God continues to speak, gradually Moses's face becomes less taut, his demeanor less rigid as his awful fear seems to slowly drain away when he hears these heartfelt words from God, spoken with a more gentle tone:

"I have surely seen the affliction of my people which are in Egypt, and have heard their cry by reason of their taskmasters; for I know their sorrows; and I am come down to deliver them out of the hand of the Egyptians, and to bring them up out of that land unto a good land and a large, unto a land flowing with milk and honey; unto the place of the Canaanites, and the Hittites, and the Amorites, and the Perizzites, and the Hivites, and the Jebusites. Now therefore, behold, the cry of the children of Israel is come unto me: and I have also seen the oppression wherewith the Egyptians oppress them. Come now therefore, and I will send thee unto Pharaoh, that thou may bring forth my people, the children of Israel, out of Egypt." (Exodus 3:7-10)

No doubt for the first time in his life Moses is seeing another side of God: The Almighty God cares for his people. He is like a caring shepherd, seeking greener pastures for his people. Soon Moses will come to the realization that He is not only the God of judgment, but He is the God of love. Faith always grows with the revelation of the love of God. Moses's faith will now increase, like every believer, as the awareness of the love of God increases; You can see an instant change in his demeanor. Moses seems less fearful. As faith increases, fear must necessarily decrease.

Walking by Faith

As you watch Moses, who seems so completely inadequate for the great task of leading the Children of Israel from the bondage of slavery in Egypt to the promised land in Canaan, you simply cannot understand why the Great Shepherd of mankind would send Jethro's worn- out shepherd on such a mission. Certainly, the all-knowing God knows Moses's resume: Prince of Egypt, murderer, fugitive; now a lowly shepherd, weak, weary, and worn- an old man carrying the burden of many years. Obviously, he is more a burnt out star than a rising star; just a burnt out shepherd who has long past his prime. He seems to have even less potential than the average or ordinary shepherd. And yet he is given such an extraordinary undertaking. Why? Why would God choose him?

Moses seems to be thinking like you, so he asks, "Who am I that I should go unto Pharaoh, and that I should bring forth the children of Israel out of Egypt?"

But God answers, "Certainly I will be with thee; and this shall be a token unto thee, that I have sent thee: When thou hast brought forth the people out of Egypt, ye shall serve God upon this mountain."

As you now listen to these words of God to Moses, you are beginning to understand their implication for the first time. God is teaching Moses to walk by faith. With faith in God's promise, nothing is impossible. Moses is about to learn the lesson of faith: "It is not by might, nor by power, but by my Spirit, says the Lord." (Zechariah 4:6) Even someone like Moses– eighty years old, and without any apparent potential– can be used by God to do mighty and powerful deeds.

The Great I Am

Moses then asks God a question that seems to suggest that he is aware of the apostasy or the falling away from faith of the children of Israel, living in Egypt for the past four hundred years. "Behold when I come unto the children of Israel, and shall say unto them, 'The God of your fathers hath sent me unto you,' and they shall say unto me, 'What is His name?' What shall I say unto them?"

The implication in his question seems obvious to you: the children of Israel believe in other gods; therefore, it would be necessary for God to identify himself to them by name.

God answers, "I AM THAT I AM: Thus shalt thou say unto the children of Israel, I am hath sent me to you."

With this response of God, it is clear to you that he does not have to distinguish himself by name from false gods or nonexistent gods; he is the one and only true God. False gods do not exist in reality– only in the vain imagination of idol worshipers. But the true God embodies reality. Then he reveals to Moses the name with which he has chosen to identify himself with his people, who no longer remember his true identity.

"Thus shalt thou say unto the children of Israel, the Lord God of your fathers, the God of Abraham, the God of Isaac, and the God of Jacob, hath sent me unto you: this is my name for ever, and this is my memorial unto all generations."

As you listen to the words of God, it suddenly occurs to you why the children of Israel where chosen by God. They were chosen to identify the one true God in a world that had lost the knowledge of God due to their unbelief. Indeed, they were chosen as a light to all Gentile nations. But after four hundred years in Egypt, their light has become dimmed by the darkness of Egypt- they became out of touch with reality- and they have forgotten the God of Abraham, the God of Isaac, and the God of Jacob.

While God is speaking, you can see how the bellowing tongues of fire seem to leap up from the burning bush with every word he utters. Also, the leaves of the burning bush are becoming increasingly animated. You have become increasingly mesmerized by the sound of the thunderous voice of God. His words resonate deep within you, touching your heart, mind, and soul. You are now feeling a holy passion for the Great Shepherd of mankind. For several minutes you continue listening to the voice of God thundering from the burning bush as he gives Moses detailed instructions about how to declare to the elders of the children of Israel how he will deliver them from the bondage of slavery in Egypt.

Shock and Awe

The response of Moses to God's commandment to go to Egypt is most enlightening about his mind-set at this time. His faith in God at this point in his life seems extremely weak. He expresses serious doubts about succeeding in convincing the Hebrews to follow him as their leader. Moses, with obvious anxiety about his mission says:

"But, behold, they will not believe me, nor hearken unto my voice: for they will say, 'The Lord hath not appeared unto thee.'"

You are feeling deeply disappointed about Moses' response to God. It is clear to you now that at this stage in his spiritual development, he is not very different from the people he is called to lead. Moses, like the Hebrews, seems reluctant to trust God completely. And like the Hebrews, it will have to take shock and awe–signs and wonders- to convince Moses to answer the call of God upon his life.

His walk of faith seems unsteady and uncertain. He is like a baby learning to walk for the first time. Clearly, Moses has yet not learned the spiritual lesson of all people of faith– "you must walk by faith and not by sight."

For several more minutes, you listen to the voice of thunder patiently explaining to Moses that success in his mission is not based on his ability, but on his availability for God to use him. If Moses should make himself available as God's servant, then God's power would be manifested. The Lord reveals to him that he would bring about irrefutable signs and wonders that would soften the hard, stony hearts of unbelief in the children of Israel. Moses would become God's prophet of shock and awe.

In His great wisdom, God knew that Moses at this time in his life is incapable of walking by faith, just like the children of Israel. Moses, like the people of his time, walks by sight only, not by faith. So what does God do in his wisdom? The same shock and awe that God told Moses he will use on the children of Israel and on Pharaoh to soften their hearts of unbelief, he now uses on Moses.

The Lord asks, "What is in your hand?"

Moses answers, "A rod."

"Cast it on the ground," the Lord commands.

Moses casts the rod on the ground. Immediately there is an incredible transformation of the rod. It becomes a moving, writhing serpent. You see the startled shepherd leaping away from the serpent. The venomous-looking reptile begins to creep menacingly on the ground toward where you are seated on the rock. Although you know the sequence of events in this biblical account, you find yourself cringing with fear as you watch the snake slithering toward you.

"Put forth your hand and take it by the tail," the Lord says.

You see how Moses, with great trepidation, reaches down with his trembling hand. You wonder if Moses' obedience is due to a greater fear of God than his fear of the serpent. The color of his face turns ashen with fear. With no less than a great force of will, he lunges down with his hand and manages to catch the snake by the tail. And it becomes a rod again.

Then the billowing fire in the burning bush gushes upward to its highest point as you hear the thunderous voice of God declaring, "That they may believe that the Lord God of their fathers, the God of Abraham, the God of Isaac and the God of Jacob, hath appeared unto you. Put now your hand into thy bosom."

Moses places his hand in his bosom. But there is a look of horror on his face when he pulls it out to look upon it. His hand is as white as snow, covered with the dread disease of leprosy.

God says, "Put now your hand in thy bosom again."

Moses, in obedience, put his hand in his bosom for a second time. Then he again takes out his hand from his bosom and examines it with an expression of relief on his face. The hand is no longer leprous, but it is normal as before.

God's voice of thunder is again heard from the midst of the burning bush. "And it shall come to pass that if they will not believe you, nor hearken to the voice of the first sign, then they will believe the voice of the latter sign. And it shall come to pass if they do not believe these two signs, neither hearken to thy voice, then thou shalt take of the water of the river, and pour it upon the dry land, and the water which thou take out of the river shall become blood upon the dry land."

While God is speaking, the words of these two verses of Scripture again come to your mind: "You must walk by faith and not by sight," and "Without faith no one can please God." You can see clearly why the present generation of the children of Israel who are born in Egypt will never make it to the Promised Land: They are without faith. They are unable to make any connection to God, because they are lacking in faith. These words spoken by God at the burning bush, promising signs and wonders, clearly reveal their fatal spiritual flaw: they walk by sight only, and not by faith.

Walking by sight, relying on signs and wonders, will be used only as a push-start measure by God that will take them out of Egypt. But it will take faith to go through the wilderness, to cause the walls of Jericho to tumble down before them, and to finally reach the Promised Land. The Bible teaches that only the next generation of the Israelites will reach the Promise Land, because unlike the present generation they will learn to walk by faith after forty years of wandering in the wilderness.

Unfortunately, for this generation of the children of Israel," seeing is believing," therefore they have to first see signs and wonders in order to believe and to follow the God of their fathers. And although they will follow God with signs and wonders, their heart will be far from God. To follow God with your heart you first have to trust him, even when you cannot see any sign of him.

Followers of God understand so well that believing is seeing.

God's Anger at Unbelief

Now you cringe under the shock of your rude awakening to Moses' glaring lack of faith, despite the promises of Almighty God. Moses, whining and complaining before God, says, "O my Lord, I am not eloquent, neither heretofore, nor since thou hast spoken unto thy servant, but I am slow in speech, and of a slow tongue."

Again the Lord thunders from the burning bush. "Who hath made man's mouth? Or who makes the dumb and the deaf, or the seeing and the blind? Have not I the Lord? Now, therefore, go and I will be with thy mouth, and teach thee what thou shalt say."

How could anyone doubt such a promise from God? But Moses replies, "O my Lord, send I pray thee by the hand of him whom thou wilt send."

Suddenly, there is an eruption of billowing flames from the burning bush when the Lord begins to speak again. You realize that God is now angry with Moses. Like the anger of a father toward a disobedient child, so the anger of the Lord is kindled against Moses who still doubts despite the assurances God has given him. Moses, in his self-centeredness, still cannot see that God requires only his availability to serve him, not his ability.

Then the moment of truth dawns upon you. Under the glaring light of self-awareness you are now seeing how truly weak your faith has been. How often you have doubted God's Word! Too often you have stumbled, and grieved the Holy Spirit by your lack of faith. You now whisper a prayer to God, asking for His forgiveness.

The voice of God thunders, "Is not Aaron, the Levite, thy brother? I know that he can speak well. And also behold he cometh to meet thee, and when he sees thee, he will be glad in his heart. And thou shalt speak unto him, and put words in his mouth, and I will be with thy mouth, and with his mouth, and will teach you what ye shall do. And he shall be thy spokesman unto the people, and he shall be, even he shall be unto thee instead of a mouth, and thou shalt be unto him instead of God. And thou shalt take this rod in thy hand, wherewith thou shalt do signs."

This time when God ceases to speak, the flame of fire in the burning bush abruptly disappears. Moses remains kneeling, unsure whether his encounter with God has come to an end. Finally, he looks around stupefied, conscious of the sudden silence and the deepening darkness.

A New Beginning

During the encounter with God, the glorious sunset over the horizon was replaced with a full moon and bright stars, twinkling in the dark night sky above. Moses stares on the bush that was burning only moments ago. There is absolutely no trace of burning now on its luxuriant leaves, glistening in the moonlight. The leaves on the bush are now stilled and unmoving. Moses lifts his head to look upward with searching eyes into the night sky; the black dome of heaven glitters with bright, shining stars.

He places his hands on his head and slowly bows his head to the ground three times in deep reverence. Then he lies flat on his stomach, his body prostrate on the rocky slope, with feet together and hands stretched out on either side– his body in the shape of a cross Moses is now still and unmoving, like the leaves on the bush that no longer burn; he seems to be in a trance. Then after a long while, in a plaintive voice, he begins praying with great fervency and with deep emotion. His words gushes from him, like a fire shut up in his bones. Moses prays in a loud voice for a long while, crying out to God with deep passion. Finally, when his voice becomes too hoarse to continue, he ceases to pray. He lies motionless as if drained of all energy.

Moses remains in the same position for a very long time, lying on the ground without moving. Then, turning his head to look on the rod lying beside him, he reaches for the rod to hold it close to his body. This rod of God only a little while ago was a writhing, hissing, hideous serpent. The thought of the rod morphing into the serpent and then the serpent morphing into the rod now fills your mind. How ironic, it seems now to you, that Moses' rod, which supported him, thus becoming an extension of himself, became his nemesis when he threw it down. It became a serpent threatening him with the sting of death.

As you reflect on how the rod will be used by Moses to cause the awful plagues upon Egypt, the mystery of good and evil comes to your mind. Moses' rod will bring the sting of death to the Egyptians, but it will bring life and liberty to the children of Israel; evil to the Egyptian, but good to the children of Israel. And the thought comes to your mind, "out of evil comes forth good." Indeed, it is as the Bible teaches, "All things work together for good to them who are called unto His holy purpose."

Then, finally rising up from the rocky ground, Moses stands up and looks upward; again his eyes search the starry sky. You notice how his face seems to glow in the darkness as if the light of the fire in the burning bush is still upon him. There is now a serene expression on his face and a calm assurance in his demeanor. Looking downward on the vast plain below, he sees the white forms of the sheep scattered in the darkness. He begins to walk briskly down the rocky slope of the mountain. With remarkable alacrity for an old man, he leaps over large boulders of rock on his way down the mountainside, and he quickly descends the mountain to the plains below. No longer is Moses, weak, weary and worn.

Reaching the base of the mountain, Moses seems greatly energized, running across the grassy plain in the direction of the sheep. The white forms of the sheep can be seen through the darkness; they are scattered along the base of the mountain. The striking contrast which you now see in his appearance, movement and demeanor, compared to when you first saw him is quite remarkable. Before his encounter at the burning bush, he appeared to you to be weak, weary, and worn; a man struggling to carry the burden of too many years. But now, after his encounter with God, you can see how he is full of vitality, greatly energized, and moving effortlessly as if the wind is now behind his back. Moses, like the disciples on the Day of Pentecost, has been given a mission, and it seems that like the disciples he is starting to experience God's abundant life- the purpose driven life- when every moment becomes precious moments to live life to its fullest.

It is evident to you that Moses is presently filled with the Holy Spirit, like the disciples after their spiritual encounter on the Day of Pentecost. The Holy Spirit, who enables ordinary men to do extraordinary things beyond their wildest imagination, has energized Moses and will empower him to perform miraculous signs and wonders. And through the Holy Spirit, the divine teacher, Moses will learn how to walk with God- walking by faith and not by sight. As Israel's greatest leader, he will begin to usher in a new age of spiritual enlightenment in the ancient world- a world that is utterly lost in spiritual darkness.

It seems clear to you that Moses will no longer just aimlessly drift through life; he is now driven by a purpose and a cause. As you reflect on your mission in life and your purpose for living, you suddenly have another rude awakening. Ruefully, you realize that like so many people your purpose for living has been more about you and less about God.

Indeed, you are now realizing that your mission in life should be greater than merely achieving the American dream, or greater than climbing the ladder of success. Now you are beginning to see how your materialistic values, which negate faith in God, seek only after selfish gain instead of selfless giving. You can see how it is draining your life away, leaving you weak, weary and worn– ultimately crushing you in mind and spirit. A life devoid of any real and lasting purpose is a life without meaning. As you reflect on Moses' encounter, you are beginning to feel an urgency to find the real purpose for your life– an urgency to serve a cause greater than yourself.

Looking down at the base of the mountain you watch as Moses quickly rounds up the scattered sheep and now begins to wend his way home. But now he will no longer be the shepherd of his father-in-law's sheep; he has become a shepherd of God's sheep. His task now is to round up all the sheep of God's pasture, the children of Israel, and lead them from Egypt to the Promised Land.

Rising up from the large boulder of rock where you have been seated, breathlessly observing Moses' encounter with God, you walk over toward the edge of the rocky mountain slope. You stand there for a long while, watching the renewed and reenergized shepherd leading the sheep of his father-in-law, Jethro. You steadfastly watch Moses, with the flock of sheep, as he moves farther and farther away into the distance. You stand there watching until they are swallowed up in the darkness of the night. But tomorrow when the sun rises, Moses will begin his long journey as the shepherd of God's chosen people. It is a journey that will take him from Egypt, through the Red Sea and through the wilderness to the Promised Land.

Looking upward to view the night sky, you see a myriad of stars, their countless points of light glittering in the darkness. You remember God's promise to Abraham: "I will make your seed as numerous as the stars in heaven." Indeed, God has kept his promise. The seed of Abraham, numbering in the millions, as the slaves of Egypt, now await Moses, the deliverer. Soon a nation will be born.

Reflecting on the history of the Jews, you wonder about the uniqueness of God's chosen people- the most blessed, yet the most persecuted and hated; the most influential, yet the most ancient people on the face of the earth. As the chosen people of God, they have been truly a light and a blessing to the Gentiles. God's chosen people have become countless points of light glittering in the darkness of the world. Indeed, God has used the Jews to lead the Gentile people to the one true God. Although they rejected their Messiah, they still remain God's chosen people. And God will never reject His own people. The Bible teaches that just as Moses returned to Egypt to deliver His chosen people, Jesus will also return from heaven to deliver them. And they will put their trust in Jesus, their Messiah.

Realizing that the time has come for you to go back to the future, you turn your eyes toward heaven again to look one last time on the glittering stars in the night sky. As you view the countless points of light embedded in the blackness of space, a feeling of peace and serenity washes over you. Indeed, it was truly good for you to be here- to witness through the eyes of your imagination Moses' encounter with God. Now, almost reluctantly, you close the eyes of your imagination. And in a flash you are back. Here you are again in the present, but certainly not the same.

The vision of the burning bush has left a deep yearning in your heart to become more than what you have been. You feel certain that the images in your mind, shaped by God's word and guided by his Spirit, were tantamount to a spiritual encounter with God; an encounter that has deeply impacted you. And you are left now feeling a burning desire to let go and let God.

Lessons Learned in Odyssey

The purpose-driven life, like the life of Moses and other men of God, after they answered the call of God, becomes a burning passion, like fire shut up in your bones. It is a consuming passion to help others, and to be used by God. Every follower of Christ should live the purpose-driven life, having a passionate desire– a holy fire that is burning within them– to become God's hand extended, and to do what they have never dared to do before; to walk by faith and not by sight.

Everyone who is truly called by God will have the desire to experience the purpose-driven life- to be taken by the Spirit to where they have never been before. Indeed, a life that is not purpose-driven- devoid of any real and lasting purpose - is a life without meaning. Life without Christ at the center is a futile, fruitless life.

Another lesson from the life of Moses teaches us how to answer the call of God. When God calls us for a certain mission, he always gives us the ability to accomplish the mission. Therefore, God does not need our ability because he gives us the ability. How do we answer the call to serve? We answer the call simply by giving to God our availability to serve. Our availability to serve God in any capacity is all that God requires. We should never feel that we are unable to serve God, because he never calls us without first equipping us to answer his call. God asks us, not for our ability to serve, but for our availability to serve him.

Timely Visit with Elijah: You Are There

The following is based on the account of the life of Elijah that can be found in 1 Kings 19:1-18.

"And after the fire came a still, small voice." (1 Kings 19:12)

Enter again the time machine of your mind to make a timely visit to the time of Elijah, Israel's greatest prophet. In the same way that you visited the time of Moses when you traveled mentally back in time, you can now visit the time of Elijah, the prophet, who was also a great miracle worker like Moses.

With the eyes of your imagination, you can witness Elijah's awesome encounter with God as you take a mental journey back to the distant past to share with Elijah his life-changing divine encounter. Yes, at that momentous time and in that most holy place, you can be there to listen to the still, small voice of God whispering to Elijah. So get ready for a thrilling adventure into the distant past through the unforgettable voyage of the mind. When you are truly guided by God's word, the voyage of the mind could become for you a voyage of discovery.

Prepare to make your timely visit by first reading the biblical account of Elijah's ministry to Israel, and once again prayerfully meditate upon God's words. And with the speed of thought and the power of imagination, the mind will transport you to the time and place of Elijah's encounter, when he heard the still, small voice of God. His awesome encounter with God was upon Mount Horeb, the same mountain where Moses first encountered God at the burning bush.

Allow the biblical account of God's word (1 Kings 19) to guide your mind as you visit the past. Now focus your mind on this mind-boggling event somewhere in Israel, far, far away, and sometime in the past, long, long ago. Imagine the place in Israel, Mount Horeb, and the time in the past, about 900

BC. Mentally, you are here now. Open wide the eyes of your imagination to see what you can see. And let your heart lead you to feel what you can feel.

The Weeping Prophet

It is a moonlit night, and you feel a soft, cool breeze caressing your face. Turning to look upward, you see a full moon with stars glittering in the night sky. You are standing on a rocky slope close to the top of Mount Horeb. The mountainous and humongous wilderness of rocks around you is bathed in the warm glow of the moonlight. The surrounding landscape far below is drenched in the soft, warm moon glow. You are near the top of the mountain, much higher than you were when on this same mountain you visited Moses, who lived several hundred years before the time of Elijah.

Standing near the summit of Mount Horeb, you can see in the moonlight the vast plain far below stretching out for miles to the far horizon.

The dark night sky over Mount Horeb is filled with the bright stars that you remember seeing when you visited Moses at the burning bush ages ago before the time of Elijah.

On the far horizon, you can see what appear to be dark storm clouds gathering; these clouds seem to be moving rapidly toward Mount Horeb. You wonder how long it will take before the storm clouds envelope the night sky, obliterating the moon and the stars, and plunging the surrounding landscape into utter darkness. You feel a sudden chill in the air as a cold wind sweeps by, and you begin to shiver in the cold. While standing there viewing the threatening storm clouds, you hear a faint sound somewhere nearby. Listening intently, you can hear the sound of someone moaning and groaning.

The sound seems to be coming from a short distance above the place where you are standing. Moving in the direction of the sound, you begin climbing the steep mountainside, making your way around large boulders of rock. The faint sound of crying grows more audible and distinct as you climb your way up the mountain. It is a groaning, moaning voice of a man weeping piteously, a sound of deep anguish.

In the bright moonlight, directly above, you can see a large dark hole in the side of the mountain just beyond a massive boulder of rock,. Climbing up the steep mountain side to get closer, you are able to see that the hole, surrounded by granite crags gleaming in the moonshine, is the mouth of a cave. Entering the opening, your attention is drawn to a flickering light behind a huge rock in the far corner of the cave. It is from there the sound of the awful groaning is coming.

The groaning echoes throughout the cave with a heart-wrenching sound. You move toward the light in the far corner of the cave, and going around the huge rock, you see a man hunched over and seated on a rock before a small fire. The fire is ablaze with the burning embers of small, dry branches.

The weeping prophet, Elijah! Holding his head with both hands, his face stained with tears, Elijah is rocking himself back and forth in a mournful lament. He is crying out plaintively like a child trying to get the attention of his mother. A cry for help? You wonder. Suddenly, you realize he is actually praying, crying out to God with this heart wrenching, mournful lament.

After shivering in the cold, you relish the warmth of the fire as you seat yourself across from Elijah; but the sight of the discouraged prophet is having a chilling effect upon you. The light of the flickering flames reveals the deep lines of anguish on his face. It is with no little surprise that you view the appearance of the man sitting across from you; he does not fit the image that you have always had of Elijah. Like the other mental journeys you have taken, you are realizing once again that perhaps you are not in complete control of your imagination. The thought that your imagination has a mind of its own, you find to be almost amusing. But at the same time quite sobering.

You have always imagined the prophet Elijah to be a fierce- looking old man, with long scraggly beard and with fiery red ruffled hair, tossed about on head and shoulder like the wild- looking mane of a lion. But the young man that you are now looking at through the new and different eyes of your imagination appears to be only in his late twenties. He has hairy skin, with extremely long dark brown hair covering his body. The hair on his head is of moderate length, and he has a full-length beard. The belt around his waist appears just as the Bible describes it, large like a girdle and made of leather. He is wearing a garment made from camel's hair.

The mantle of Elijah, having a dark-blue color, is cast aside and thrown carelessly on the floor of the cave some distance away from him. According to the Bible his mantle, like Moses's rod, is holy and anointed by God, representing the power of God to perform miracles. However, it is surprisingly lying several feet away from him, discarded on the stony ground. The mantle seems the furthest thing from his mind at the moment.

It is clear to you that you are seeing a burnt-out prophet, utterly hopeless and powerless. With the realization that you are witnessing Elijah at the lowest point in his life, you wonder about the cause that has brought Israel's greatest prophet to this valley of despair on top of this mountain, Mount Horeb.

From Mount Carmel, where he called down fire from heaven and then slew the prophets of the false god Baal after first shutting up the heavens over Israel from giving rain for three years, this mighty man of God has descended to this dark valley of fear and despair. What caused the great faith of this prophet of God to falter? Only recently he ran for his life in fear from the wicked queen Jezebel. What shattered the faith of this spiritual giant who became so depressed and hopeless on his way to this mountain that he asked God to take his life? Suddenly, it occurs to you that the same troubling questions are now probably weighing heavily on the heart of the weeping prophet, Elijah.

Perhaps he is weeping with the same shame and guilt like Peter, who wept bitterly when he denied Christ three times. When he became afraid, Peter found himself no longer "walking in the power of the Spirit," but walking in the weakness of the flesh. Suddenly this verse of scripture now comes to your mind, "the spirit is willing, but the flesh is weak." Indeed, this is applicable not only to Elijah and Peter, but to so many of the spiritual giants of the Bible such as Abraham, Jacob, Moses, David, and so many Christians who all failed to walk consistently in the power of the Holy Spirit.

Perhaps this could be the reason for Elijah's faltering faith: Walking in the weakness or the passion of the flesh. The great prophet, Elijah "born in sin and shaped in iniquity" like the rest of humanity, walked with feet of clay that crumbled when the going got tough. It appears that from time to time Elijah like Peter and so many believers– all with feet of clay– neglected to walk in the Spirit but walked in the flesh instead. Therefore they stumbled and fell in their walk with the Lord.

You now remember the time when Peter walked on water. It is evident to you that Elijah is now walking like how Peter walked when he began to sink. Peter walked on water in the power of the Spirit with his eyes staying on Jesus. But when he took his eyes off Jesus and saw the boisterous waves, he sank in the churning bellows–the weakness of the flesh. No doubt, Elijah came to the place where he took his eyes off God and could see only his great nemesis, the threatening pagan queen, Jezebel. And like Peter he sank: Into the valley of fear and despair he sank.

As you watch the tearful, gloomy prophet looking so discouraged, this thought crosses your mind: as long as Elijah was on the offense, zealous for God, and fighting the good fight of faith, there was no fear, and miracles followed. But in self-defense, his focus turned on himself due to the threats of Jezebel, so he became fearful and could do no miracles. Indeed, you must be either on the offense for God, or on the defense for self; you cannot do both at the same time. Walking in the Spirit is walking in faith and in power; walking in the flesh is walking in fear and weakness.

As you sit there observing Elijah, you can see that this mighty man of God is no different from you, or any man; indeed, he is as the Bible describes him to be, "a man of like passions." We all walk with feet of clay. The Bible teaches that the arms of flesh will fail us every time.

Gradually, the passionate groaning and weeping of the troubled prophet subsides. Only the crackling sound of the dried branches burning in the fire can be heard now. He opens his eye, bloodshot red with crying, and turns his head, glancing fleetingly on his mantle. He sees it on the far side of the cave, thrown carelessly down on the floor of the cave.

Feeling the cold, he rubs his hands together, shivering. He gets up from his seat before the fire and walks over to the mantle and picks it up.

Suddenly, he pauses in the act of picking up the mantle, listening intently. Hearing a sound outside the cave, he drops the mantle on the rock and hurriedly makes his way through the entrance of the cave, stopping a few feet outside the entrance. He stands there looking around in the moonlight.

Leaving your warm seat before the fire, you follow him to the entrance. Like Elijah, you look outside around the area of the entrance, but you see nothing but large boulders and rocks gleaming in the moonlight. Then you hear the most soothing, sweetest sound– a gently rumbling melodious voice. At once you identify the sound as the voice of God.

But his voice is quite different now from the voice you heard, while visiting Moses at the burning bush. It occurs to you that God is aware of Elijah's emotional condition so the tone of his voice with Elijah is different. Not surprisingly, the language is unknown to you. The language at that time in Israel is Hebrew. But you know exactly what God is saying to Elijah; You are feeling glad now that you took the time to read the conversation between God and Elijah in your Bible just before making your visit to this time and place.

"What are you doing here, Elijah?" the voice of God asks softly and tenderly. However, his words seem to be in the form of a statement than a question. It is soothing, like the voice of a mother as she comforts her hurting child. His warm, comforting voice surrounds and enfolds you; it seems to be coming from every direction.

Elijah falls to his knees. Looking up toward heaven, he answers God, his face gloomy with discouragement and his voice shaking with emotion, "I have been very jealous for the Lord God of hosts, for the children of Israel have forsaken thy covenants, thrown down thy altars, and slain thy prophets with the sword, and I, even I only am left; and they seek my life to take it away."

There is a long pause. Elijah steadfastly is looking toward heaven. Softly and tenderly, the voice of God is heard once again. "Go forth and stand upon the mount before the Lord."

Elijah turns his head to look up at the steep side of the mountain. He sees a gigantic rock situated close to the top of Mount Horeb. He begins climbing up the steep mountain side, heading straight for the rock. He quickly makes his way up the side of the mountain, and reaching the top, he climbs on the rock. But instead of standing on the mountain as the Lord commanded him, he sits on the rock. Folding his arms, he waits to hear from God.

You wonder how the Lord will deal with this fearful and powerless prophet. You now remember vividly how the weak, weary, and worn-out prophet, Moses, was transformed by God on Mount Horeb through signs and wonders. The burning bush, the rod becoming a snake, and his hand turning white with leprosy seemed to have a transforming effect upon Moses. Like Moses at that time, Elijah is now before God on the same mountain, Mount Horeb. How will the signs and wonders that Elijah is about to witness rekindle his faith and renew his spiritual strength? You watch and wait to see what will happen.

The Wind

Suddenly, the mountain is enveloped in thick darkness, the moon and the stars vanishing: the night sky covered by swift-moving black clouds. The storm clouds on the horizon, which you saw before now blanket the sky, looking ominous and foreboding. Also, there is a sudden freezing cold, causing you to shiver. Then the sudden blast of a strong wind causes you to retreat closer to the mouth of the cave. Looking upward, you can see high above a dark funnel-shaped cloud descending. Your heart leaps within you as you watch a tornado looming in the darkness. The terrible- looking twister seems to be descending straight to where Elijah is sitting on the rock.

In the darkness, you can barely see the form of Elijah as he hurriedly climbs down from the rock. With remarkable speed and agility, he hurriedly makes his way down the side of the mountain and rushes into the cave, where you are now safely huddled behind a rock. Reaching the refuge of the cave, he moves into its interior to stand at a location close enough to the entrance of the cave. From this vantage point in the cave, he watches the slowly descending funnel-shaped cloud.

The intensity of the wind is increasing as the tornado descends; The sound is now almost deafening. The horrible sound of the twister is like the sound of a freight train rumbling on top of Mount Horeb. Moving from behind the rock to stand near Elijah, you look out through the opening of the cave; you can see the frightening spectacle of the tornado's wild fury. It is unbelievably frightening; the tornado is moving down toward the cave. It is as if the mountain is about to be torn apart by the incredible force of the wind. You can feel now the unbearable force of the wind starting to blow through the wide mouth of the cave. You grab hold of a large boulder to keep from being dashed against the side of the cave by the wind.

With wonder and amazement, you watch as the tornado descends to within a few feet above the rock, where Elijah was seated. Hovering above the rock, the funnel shaped twister seems to be targeting the rock on which Elijah had been sitting before, while waiting to hear from God. Then the rock literally explodes before your eyes, shattering into pieces. Seeing what is happening, Elijah falls to his knees, overcome with terror. He crouches behind the rock on which his mantle is draped. While crouching there, his hand inadvertently touches the hem of the mantle. And what happens next is utterly surreal!

Now you are struck by an unbelievably strange occurrence. As you look through the wide entrance of the cave, the sight and sound of the tornado's destructive fury is only too evident. But inexplicably, inside the cave the air now is stilled, unmoving, not even the slightest breeze is felt. It is as if an invisible door at the entrance is shutting out the force of the wind. You find such a surreal occurrence to be extremely puzzling. Elijah also is watching in bewilderment. Getting up from where he was crouched when his hand touched the hem of the mantle, he begins to move cautiously to the entrance to investigate the apparent checkpoint of the tornado. But as soon as he moves away from the mantle, the invisible door against the wind is blown wide open. The force of the wind enters the cave once again with a vengeance.

A mighty blast of rushing wind sends him reeling backward, slipping and sliding until he is flat on his back. Elijah is blown by the mighty, rushing wind, rolling over and over on the stony ground of the cave, until he is pinned against the side of the cave. The extremely powerful force of the wind fills the cave; there is no escape. Elijah wraps his arms around a large rock to keep from being blown away outside the cave. Now the wind begins to blow in an uncanny manner like the suction of a vacuum. The force of the wind is pulling at you, as if to dislodge you from the cave. Hugging the rock protruding from the side of the cave, you strain with every ounce of strength against the force of the wind in order not to be blown away. Without your anchor, the solid rock on which you are holding, you feel sure that you would either be dashed against the wall of the cave, or be sucked out of the cave to be dashed to pieces on Mount Horeb.

Across from you on the other side, Elijah is also straining to hold onto his rock. But he seems to be losing his grip on the rock due to the force of the unrelenting wind. He is gripped with fear, his face is livid with a look of terror. He notices the smaller rock close by on which his mantle is draped, around which he could wrap his hand to anchor himself inside the cave. It strikes you as extremely strange that the mantle is not blown away from the rock by the incredible force of the wind. It seems as if it is somehow fastened to the rock. Despite the mighty rushing wind, the mantle remains unruffled, undisturbed.

Reaching his right hand to grab the rock on which the mantle is draped, Elijah's hand inadvertently touches the mantle for a second time.

At the exact moment when the mantle is touched by his hand, the wind suddenly stops. But this time the relentless force of the wind abruptly stops not only inside the cave but outside as well. The awful fury, the powerful force and the deafening sound of the whirlwind are now over; silence, stillness; peace returns to Mount Horeb. But even so, your aching arms remain cleaved to the rock that you have been holding onto for dear life. You slumped limply beside the rock; you feel terribly shaken, completely drained, and utterly breathless by the horrific experience of the dreadful wind.

You can hear the heavy breathing of Elijah, who is also motionless. You watch the movement of his heaving chest while he is breathing heavily. Like you, he is trying to catch his breath, which was taken away not only by the intensity of the wind but by the sheer terror of the windstorm. Indeed, this wind was breathtaking in more ways than one.

Finally, you hear Elijah stirring. You see him getting up and then moving slowly toward the entrance of the cave– his chest heaving as he takes deep gulps of air. Unwrapping your arms from around the rock that you have been hugging during the windstorm, you get up slowly and carefully. Gingerly you walk over to the entrance where Elijah remains standing.

Standing beside him, you look through the opening of the cave at the night sky to see the remnants of the funnel-shaped cloud now becoming long, tiny fragments of wispy clouds that quickly vanish away. Looking high above, you can see the dark blanket of cloud also quickly dispersing, revealing again the twinkling stars in the dark night sky and the moon shining in its glorious splendor. But on Elijah's face, you see a dark expression of gloom and a haunting fear. Certainly for Elijah, his spiritual struggle continues. God is not finished with Elijah yet. You can see that his doubts and confusion still remain.

Although it seems clear to you that this was a supernatural encounter evidenced by the mighty display of God's power, nevertheless, according to the biblical account, God was not in the windstorm. Why? Perhaps it is because for the faithful believer, the presence of God is always a joyful, healing and life-giving phenomenon; It seems to you that perhaps God withdrew his presence in order to test Elijah, just like how Jesus tested his disciples. The Bible reveals that the disciples became fearful like Elijah, when Jesus was asleep on a boat with them in the midst of a storm on the Sea of Galilee. They cried out to Jesus, "Master, don't you care that we perish?" Looking on Elijah's anxious and troubled face marred with doubt, you can hear ringing in your ears the words of Jesus spoken to his disciples after he calmed the storm: "O ye of little faith. Why are ye so afraid?" (Mark 4:37-41). Like Elijah, they failed their test. Instead of stepping out in faith, they cringed with fear.

Clearly, Elijah's faith is still very weak. It seems evident that his lack of faith is the reason for his fear and deep depression. The Bible reveals that Elijah ran for his life when Jezebel threatened to kill him. Could it be that the strength of his faith was shorn by Jezebel's threat to take his life? Indeed, it seems to you now that Elijah's faith has been weakened by Jezebel's threat, like Samson became weakened by Delilah's deceit when she cut off his hair– the visible sign of Samson's faith in God– his hope and strength. It seems that like the faithless Samson, and the faithless disciples, Elijah is going through God's faith- building crucible.

The Earthquake

While standing at the entrance of the cave musing on Elijah's crisis of faith, as well as on your own weaknesses as a person of faith, you begin to wonder about the kind of faith-building crucible that you might have to go through as you walk by faith. You realize that sooner or later you will have to go through your own test. Indeed, without a test, there is no testimony– no cross, no crown, and no pain, no gain. Indeed, the Bible says that God, our heavenly Father, chastises those whom he loves. His loving rebuke always leads to repentance. Unless we are shaken, we just can't wake up. We have to be shaken until doubts and fears give way to faith.

Suddenly, the ground beneath you begins to shake. Visibly shaken more with fright than the shaking of the earth, Elijah instantly leaps backward inside the cave and braces himself against the wall. The ground beneath is becoming as unsteady as the deck of a ship tossing on the waves of the sea. Staggering like a drunken man, you make your way back to your place of refuge, the rock on the other side of the cave. Just like before, you anchor yourself in the cave by embracing the unshakable rock with your arms. You prepare for the worse. According to the biblical record of these events, you know that after the wind then comes the earthquake.

Looking out through the wide entrance of the cave while the earth is violently shaking, you see an avalanche of rocks raining down the steep mountainside. Numerous large boulders of rocks can be seen bounding, skipping, and tumbling down from the top of Mount Horeb with maddening speed. Large boulders crash into each other with loud explosive sounds, splintering into countless small fragments of rocks. You watch with fascination the earthquake changing and reshaping the appearance of Mount Horeb right before your eyes. It occurs to you that at this moment God is in the process of changing and reshaping Elijah's spiritual condition in the same way. Bit by bit God is breaking his stony heart of doubt and fear– leading him to repentance.

Suddenly, you hear a thud on the floor of the cave behind you, followed by a loud grunt of pain. You turn to see Elijah lying sprawled on the ground. Apparently, he was dislodged from where he was braced against the wall by the violent shaking. He crawls on his hands and knees to the rock that is draped with his mantle; the same rock on which he was holding before during the windstorm. Just like before, as he reaches to hold the rock, his hand inadvertently touches the mantle. At that instant, the shaking of the earth stops, just as the windstorm stopped. However, although the shaking of the earth has stopped, you can still hear the sound of rocks rolling violently down the side of the mountain for a long while.

Finally, everywhere is quiet again. You look on the other side of the cave to see the frightened prophet lying prostrate on the ground, flat on his stomach, one hand covering his head, the other holding on to the mantle, draped over the rock. Watching this suffering man of God, it occurs to you that passing through God's crucible as he molds and reshapes you can be really painful. Certainly, this faith walk is no cake walk.

After a long while, nervously holding onto the rock with the mantle, Elijah finally decides it is now safe to get up from his prone position on the stony floor of the cave. He walks with unsteady steps, apparently badly shaken emotionally, to venture outside. Elijah moves slowly and cautiously to the entrance. He stands at the entrance of the cave where he surveys the changed appearance of Mount Horeb under the starry moonlit night sky.

You wonder what might be going through his mind right now. Certainly when he ran from Jezebel to the refuge of Mount Horeb, he did not bargain for anything like this. Perhaps he is thinking that this is like jumping out of the frying pan into the fire. And now you are struck by this thought: That's exactly what is coming next– fire! According to the record of these events in the Bible, first was the wind, and after the wind, the earthquake and after the earthquake, the fire.

You know the biblical history of the time of Elijah so well. And you know how it ends. You know how the loving God will take Elijah through this awful test. Of course, now he is completely clueless about the outcome. Indeed, the fear of the unknown makes cowards of us all. It is now becoming clear to you that since it is not possible for anyone to know anything about the future, the only way that you can experience peace in any storm is by having faith in the One who holds the future. The peace that passes all understanding is only possible when you put your trust in the One who is the shelter in a time of storm; Jesus is the Prince of Peace. Therefore, trusting in the security of God's love and power is the only way to experience lasting peace.

As you reflect on Elijah's great travail and all that he is going through, you realize that you are now getting a lesson right now about God's amazing grace. God's grace is always reaching out to connect to the faith of his people. Grace is truly amazing. According to the Bible, you cannot earn grace, nor can you ever deserve it. However, you must have a yearning for grace in order to receive it. And the yearning for grace only comes through trials and tribulations.

This yearning for God's grace seems now to you to be synonymous to faith in God. When you experience blood, sweat, and tears, and complete helplessness, and when you come to the end of your rope, then you will have a yearning for God's grace– His divine help. Through your desperate yearning, you will be moved by faith to ask, to seek, and to knock at the mercy door of God.

As you go through life, the wind blows, the earth shakes, and the fire burns, but out of the trials of life comes forth faith. Your faith is the greatest gift because it is enveloped with God's grace; faith is the gift of God's grace. And faith connects you to the love of God. There is indeed a cure from the curse of fear– an antidote for all your fears. The healing love of God is the remedy for all your fears. The Bible says, "Love casts out fear."

The Fire

Rousing yourself from musings about Elijah's awful spiritual struggles as well as your own struggles, you turn your attention to Elijah still standing at the entrance of the cave. You walk over to the entrance to stand beside him once again. In the bright moonlight, you survey the multitude of rock fragments on the mountainside in the aftermath of the wind and the earthquake. Looking on the shaken prophet, your heart goes out to him. Like Job, he is being tested and must go through God's fiery trials. And like Job, he will come forth like gold. Again, the thought enters your mind: no pain, no gain.

As you are thinking about this world's hostile spiritual environment for people of faith, you cast your eyes below to take another look down the side of the mountain. And you see the fire coming! Unaware of the fire, Elijah continues to gaze upon the stars in the night sky; apparently searching for a sign above from God. But when he finally looks down, he gasps with sudden fright. Seeing the fire moving rapidly toward the cave, he helplessly places his hands on his head, not knowing what to do or where to run. His eyes are wide with a desperate look of panic.

You see a ring of fire below, encircling the mountain. And the raging fire is heading straight up toward the cave. The flaming inferno is rapidly moving up the mountainside, engulfing with its towering flames everything in its path. The cave, which offered some protection against the wind and the earthquake, now offers little to no protection against the fire; the mouth of the cave is wide open to the devouring flames.

Unlike Elijah's previous encounters with Jezebel, the wind and the earthquake, with this encounter of the fire he has no plan of action. There is no place to run, no place to hide, and no place to take cover. Threatened by the wicked Jezebel, he could run away to Mount Horeb and find a hiding place. Blown by the fury of the wind, he could hide behind a boulder inside the cave and hope the large rock could be a shield against the wind; and jolted by the shattering upheaval of the earthquake, he could take cover in the cave and brace himself against the wall of the cave and just hang on with all his might from being thrown down the steep mountainside. But now, what can he do?

In fear and desperation, Elijah does what everyone does when everything seems hopeless. He falls to his knees and cries out to God. However, it appears that he is crying out more out of fear and desperation than from faith in God's divine protection. His prayer is not an act of faith, but a reaction from fear. When one is moved by faith, then praying to God is the first resort. But when moved by fear, praying is the last resort.

You watch the terrified prophet as he prays. He prays with eyes wide open, anxiously watching the fire. And the more he prays, the closer the fire gets. And the closer the fire gets, the more desperate he seems to become– his countenance terribly marred with hopelessness. It is quite evident to you that his prayer now can only be an exercise in futility. Prayer without faith is like a letter mailed without a stamp– it always returns to the sender. Such prayers will always return without an answer.

In the biblical account, which you read about this event, involving the wind, earthquake and fire, it is revealed that God only passed by Elijah. Why no personal connection with Elijah? Perhaps, because Elijah's faith had given way to fear; it is becoming increasingly clear to you now that without faith there can be no spiritual connection with God. Therefore, the Bible reveals that God was not in the wind, the earthquake, and the fire when Elijah was tested on Mount Horeb.

As you watch Elijah pray, you can see the awful consequences of crippling fear on the human soul. The Bible reveals that he was filled with the same fear when he ran from Jezebel and requested God to take his life. The comparison of the powerless Samson with the powerless Elijah now comes to your mind, again. Like Elijah, the power of the Spirit departed from Samson, because he lacked the faith to trust in God in his weakest moment, when tempted by Delilah (Judges 16:14). Sampson's nemesis was Delilah, and now Elijah's nemesis is Jezebel.

God's word is unequivocal about how to please him: "Without faith no man can please God." When faith is absent from the heart, the Spirit of God is also absent. No wonder God's word says, "It is not by might, nor by power, but by my Spirit, says the Lord." Indeed, without his Spirit, you are without power.

Not knowing what to do, Elijah retreats into the cave. Within minutes the flames of the fire are leaping through the wide entrance of the cave; only a miracle can save him. He retreats into the cave until his back is against the wall. He stands there looking helplessly on the flames as he feels the intense heat; a look of horror is on his face. You now ask the same question that Elijah's disciple, Elisha, asked when he separated the water of the Jordon River by using Elijah's mantle: "Where is the God of Elijah?" (2 Kings 2:14) And this resounding answer suddenly comes to you: God has never left Elijah, and he will never forsake him, but he is waiting. He is waiting for Elijah to connect again to his divine power though faith in God. God is waiting for Elijah to put his faith in action by using his mantle, the symbol of his faith in God.

As he stands there, rigid and motionless, a soul crippled with fear, the tongues of fire begin to leap into the cave. The fire is enveloping the cave and quickly closing in on him. Surprisingly, it seems that you are also feeling the intense heat. Of course, this feeling must be mind over matter, like it seemed just a little while ago when you felt the force of the wind and the violent shaking of the earthquake. What else could it be? You are here only in mind, not in body. Nevertheless, you retreat to your place of refuge in the cave: back to your rock, your hiding place from the wind, the earthquake, and now the fire.

But on Elijah's face, you see a sudden, unbelievable change. Your attention is arrested, riveted by the incredible change. In the midst of the fire, there is now a deeply thoughtful, pensive, and sobering expression on his face, as if he is experiencing a sudden awakening. He turns his head to look where the mantle is lying on the rock, his face framed with a new awareness and the deepest concern. The devouring flames are steadily creeping toward the mantle. It seems inevitable–within a matter of seconds the mantle will go up in flames. His back is against the wall, but suddenly, you see a resolute and determined look on his face. He fastens his eyes on the mantle with cool resolve in the heat of the fire. Standing in the midst of the fire, his focus now seems not on his safety but only on securing the mantle. He now seems fearless despite the unbearable heat of the fire.

The thought comes to your mind that no doubt, Elijah realizes that he no longer has the option for flight; he is left with only one option–fight the good fight of faith. Clearly, right now flight is not an option. Indeed, for a servant of God, flight should never be an option. This is what Elijah had forgotten: if God is for you, who or what can be against you.

Leaping over the flames, unmindful of the intense heat, he runs toward the rock where he left his mantle. He grabs it up from the rock and holds it tenderly for a brief moment against his chest, like a mother holding her baby. Then with the mantle in his hand, he begins to frantically beat against the flames closing in on him. Elijah beats against the fire just like how the Bible describes Samson beating the Philistines with the jawbone of a horse. He fiercely attacks the devouring flames with the mantle, shouting triumphantly while he beats down on the retreating flames.

Suddenly, it seems like an invisible stream of water is being poured out from the mantle onto the fire. As the mantle touches the flames, the fire begins to be snuffed out, dissipating to a sizzling steam. Starting from Elijah's feet, the quenching of the fire begins to spread everywhere throughout the cave. The quenching continues to spread through the entrance, and then spreads down and around the mountainside until in a matter of minutes the fire is completely gone. Only a cloud of white smoke ascending upward to the starry night sky can now be seen.

You marvel at what faith in God can do, when one acts by faith instead of cringing in fear. No wonder Jesus rebukes his disciples over and over again about their weak faith. How often Jesus expresses his deep chagrin with the disciples by saying, "O ye of little faith," "How long must I suffer your lack of faith." Jesus says, "If you have faith, the size of a little mustard seed, you can say to this mountain be removed and be cast into the sea, and it shall be done." (Matthew 17:20) A sense of guilt washes over you. And now you pray the prayer of all believers who have become cognizant of the weakness of their faith, "Lord I believe, help my unbelief."

With renewed faith, Elijah triumphantly surveys the ashes around him from the extinguished fire. Looking on the mantle in his hand, his face is suddenly enveloped with indescribable ecstasy. Then he covers his face with the mantle and begins to laugh. His shoulders shake vigorously with the kind of laughter that comes from sheer joy, a joy that bubbles over. Laughing with irrepressible joy, Elijah runs out of the cave. Standing there, he looks up toward heaven and, in a loud voice, begins to shout words in the Hebrew language. Although you do not know the language, the meaning is very evident based on his joyous and triumphant demeanor. It is obvious to you that Elijah is praising God and thanking God with all his might.

Yes, you can see so clearly now that God was not in the wind, the earthquake, nor the fire. But He was certainly in the mantle, which embodies the faith of Elijah. It is clear to you now that it was only the power of God manifested in the mantle that saved Elijah from the wind, when God so graciously allowed his hand to touch the mantle. Also, it was God's power in the mantle that saved him from the earthquake when God again so graciously allowed him to touch the mantle. Finally, it was God's grace that cornered Elijah in the fire, so that by faith he could see the power of God waiting to be unleashed through the mantle. When Elijah's back was against the wall, God graciously enabled him to take his eyes off the existing problem and focus on the solution. Faith in God is the solution to any problem. Indeed, God's power, manifested though his mercy and grace, is only released through your faith in him.

Elijah's prayer of thanksgiving, the shouting of praises to God, finally comes to an end. He now quietly kneels down. Although he is silent, it appears that he is still praying. His shoulders begin shaking once again, but not with laughter. He is weeping again. You can see his tears glistening on his cheeks in the bright moonlight. But you can also see that his tears are not caused by fear and desperation like before; there is no sound of moaning and groaning. Now, it seems that he is shedding in silence tears of repentance. He is now broken, emotionally and feeling contrite before God. No doubt, while he was praising God, he could see with greater clarity the faithfulness of God contrasted with his own weaknesses and faithlessness. It seems to you that he is crying as Peter cried when he denied Christ due to the weakness of his faith. Like Peter, he seems to be crying tears of repentance.

The Still, Small Voice

Praying for a long while, Elijah finally rises from his kneeling position and returns to the cave. He then proceeds to pick up a smooth flat stone, and places it in a corner of the cave. Covering himself with his mantle, he lies down on the floor of the cave, resting his head on the flat stone as a pillow. While leaning on the rock, which has become for you a kind of refuge and comfort zone in the cave, you eagerly wait for the next event in Elijah's life that you imagine will occur at any moment.

After lying for a while on his back, Elijah turns on his side with his face toward you. His eyes are closed and he appears to be drifting off to sleep. Suddenly, his eyes pop open. He rises up, leans on his elbow, listening intently. Then you hear a sound– a whisper– a still, small voice. There is something quite extraordinary about the sound. The soft whisper spoken in the Hebrew language sounds refreshingly soothing. It soothes like a cool, gentle breeze in the heat of the day. And in a wonderfully strange way, the whisper touches your soul with warmth like the feeling of a warm blanket on a cold night. The still, small voice refreshes and warms your soul at the same time. But just how the sweet, tender voice of the Spirit touches your innermost being is really beyond words.

Elijah seems transfixed– motionless with eyes wide with wonder, listening intently to the still, small voice for several minutes. You can see a distinct change to his countenance; his face is now framed with an expression of the deepest peace and serenity. Then getting up, he wraps his face in his mantle and walks over to the entrance of the cave. He stands there for a long time, erect and unmoving. And he waits.

Then you hear– not the sound of the still, small voice this time– but the deep, melodious rumble of the tender voice of God. The same voice that spoke to Elijah before the advent of the wind, the earthquake, and the fire. The Spirit of God asks Elijah the same question as before: "What are you doing here, Elijah?"

Elijah gave the same answer as before: "I have been very jealous for the Lord, God of hosts, because the children of Israel have forsaken thy covenant, thrown down thy altars, and slain thy prophets with the sword, and I, even I only am left, and they seek my life to take it away."

Although Elijah gave the same report to God before, there is now a striking contrast in the way that this report is delivered. The same words, but now a completely different attitude! His demeanor and attitude as he now stands before God have completely changed. Now there is not the slightest trace of fear, alarm, or self-pity as he makes his report to God. His voice is no longer shaken with emotion, and his face is no longer marred with hopelessness and despair. He now stands before God like a courageous soldier, giving his report to his commander in chief. And like a good soldier he stands there waiting– ready, willing and unafraid, trusting only in his sovereign Lord.

You hear God's commandments to Elijah in his melodious, gentle, rumbling voice. "Go, return on thy way to the wilderness of Damascus, and when thou comest anoint Hazael to be king over Syria. And Jehu the son of Nimshi shalt thou anoint to be king over Israel. And Elisha, the son of Shaphat of

Abel-Meholah shalt thou anoint to be the prophet in thy room. And it shall come to pass that him that escapes the sword of Hazael shall Jehu slay, and him that escapes from the sword of Jehu shall Elisha slay. Yet I have left me several thousand in Israel, all the knees which have not bowed unto Baal, and every mouth which hath not kissed him."

As you listen to God's commandments to Elijah, you can clearly see that God is in perfect control of the existing crisis in Israel. It is also clear that Elijah is being recalled from his mission as a prophet to Israel, and that his replacement will be Elisha. You wonder about the reason for such a change. Could the reason for the change be found in the mysterious still, small voice?

You wonder what God told Elijah in his still, small voice. While you are thinking about the possible meaning and purpose for the mysterious whisper, you move closer to where Elijah is now kneeling before the Spirit of God while he listens to his commandments.

After God ceases to speak, Elijah bows his head to the ground in worship. He remains in such a position of worship for a long while. Finally, when it becomes evident that his divine encounter with God is over, he gets up from his kneeling position, and looks up toward heaven, his eyes searching the night looking at the multitude of shining stars just like Moses gazed at the stars, when you visited him ages ago. There is a look of eagerness and excitement on his face. Taking away the mantle from around his head, he places it across his shoulders. There is the appearance of urgency and purpose in his every movement, and immediately he begins to make his way down the steep mountainside. With the strength and agility of his youthful years, he quickly descends the mountain slope, until he passes from your view.

The Traveler

You are familiar with the biblical account concerning Elijah, so you know exactly where he is now heading. In his obedience to the commandments of the Lord, Elijah is now on his way to anoint Hazael to be king over Syria, and Jehu to be king over Israel. Elijah will also find Elisha, his disciple, and he will cast his mantle upon him, anointing him as his successor as God's prophet over Israel.

Soon after anointing Elisha as his replacement, he will be caught up in the air by a whirlwind and will be taken away in a chariot of fire, drawn by horses of fire. And what will be the next spectacular event in Elijah's life? It will be his visit with Moses to talk with Jesus on the Mount of Transfiguration about nine hundred years in the future. Wonder of wonders!

It suddenly occurs to you that you are now living in the "end time," and if you live long enough, you just might get to see Elijah, the time traveler, restoring the chosen nation of Israel to God. The return of Elijah to Israel at some time in the future is prophesied by Christ Jesus, "Elijah truly shall first come and restore all things" (Matthew 17:11). The mystery of the spiritual realm is beyond comprehension to our finite minds. The divine plan to save lost humanity is truly mind boggling!

Looking down from the summit of Mount Horeb, you can see Elijah crossing the vast plains below. You now remember your mental journey to Mount Horeb, when you visited Moses so many centuries ago before the time of Elijah. At that time you also watched Moses crossing the same plains as he departed like Elijah from Mount Horeb. Although Moses and Elijah departed at a different time from Mount Horeb (Moses 1500 BC and Elijah 900 BC), yet they would arrive together at the same future time on the Mount of Transfiguration to be with Christ. Again the thought that Elijah and Moses could have been time travelers to the time of Jesus enters your mind. And again you dismiss this thought as perhaps a thought that is too speculative to entertain.

Many Bible scholars believe that from the Mount of transfiguration Elijah and Moses will travel to the future "end time," called the time of the great tribulation. During this time, they will testify about the second coming of their Messiah through signs and wonders to the last generation of the Jews. And now you are feeling a deep sense of wonder as you reflect on God's awesome plan of redemption. The amazing grace and wisdom of God's plan is so mind boggling! God has provided a way for the salvation of the Jews, his chosen people.

Soon the swiftly moving form of Elijah, walking in the distance far below, disappears from view. Now you can see only the emptiness of the vast plains. You look upward toward heaven to see a cloudless night sky. The moon is shining in its splendor, and the glittering stars looking like sparkling diamonds bedeck the dome of heaven with their heavenly light. You feel absolutely certain that the images from your mental journey to the time of Elijah will always remain with you. Indeed, it was a remarkable journey of discovery.

And now it is time; the time for you to go back has come. You came, you saw, and what you have learned in your spiritual odyssey you will now take back with you. Back to the future you must now travel. So you close the eye of your Spirit-led imagination to return to the present. And in the twinkling of an eye here you are again.

Without a doubt, you feel that this mental journey to the time of Elijah was in essence a spiritual journey for you. The presence of God was so palpable during your mental visit. Certainly, while observing the weakness and fear of Elijah, you were reminded of your own weaknesses and fears. Indeed, as you shared his encounter with God, you learned invaluable spiritual lessons that will always remain with you.

Lessons Learned in Odyssey

One of the lessons that we learned from Elijah's encounter with God is the means our heavenly Father uses to correct us, and the means he uses to bless us. Sometimes God shouts at us to get our attention through our pain as a means of correction. But at times he speaks to our hearts in his still small voice to bless us. For example, in the wind, earthquake and fire, God shouted at Elijah to get his attention as a means of correction so that Elijah could identify the spiritual need in his life. But in the whisper of the still, small voice, God in his pleasure blesses Elijah by restoring his relationship with God, restoring his ministry, and renewing his spiritual strength.

We also learned the lesson of faith. The lesson of faith is simply this: Don't focus on the problem in your life, but focus on the solution to every problem. Focus on God, only! Faith in God is the solution to any problem. Our faith in God is our spiritual mantle that connects us to the awesome power of God. And this spiritual mantle of faith gives us power, love, and a sound mind. Faith is the antidote to fear. Let us wear the mantle of faith always, and then we will walk in the power of the Holy Spirit. Indeed, "God does not give us the spirit of fear, but of power, love and a sound mind."

Timely Visit to the Birth of Jesus: You Are There

The following is based on the account of the Birth of Jesus found in Luke 2:1-20

"And suddenly there was with the angel a multitude of the heavenly host praising God." (Luke 2:13)

Perhaps like most people, you have been enthralled and thrilled by the unique sights and sounds of Christmas. Year after year, devout Christians look forward to the most celebrated day of the year: Christmas! The ubiquitous sights of Christmas lights and the joyful sounds of Christmas carols are a reflection and an echo from the past, reverberating across the canyons of time—from the first Christmas to the present time. Christmas lights are a vivid reminder of the wondrous sight of the bright shining star, and the heavenly light shining around the shepherds. Also, Christmas carols are evocative of the sound of praises from the angelic host, announcing the birth of the Christ child, Jesus.

Travel back to the past now to experience the enthralling sights and the thrilling sounds of the first Christmas. Take an imaginary journey through time to see through the eyes of the imagination the event that changed the world– the birth of Jesus. The time machine of your mind will take you to the birth of Christ, to the first Christmas, when the light of heaven pierced the darkness of the world. Not just mentally but spiritually, you can travel to a time when the sweet melodious sound of praises, which gushed from the angelic host, brought hope to the abysmal spiritual void of the world– the hope of peace and goodwill toward men. Hear the glorious message from the angelic host one more time: Emmanuel has come.

Let the Holy Spirit guide your mental journey to the first Christmas, when in the midst of the chaos and discord of fallen humanity, the world was imbued with heaven's angelic symphony, promising joy, peace, and goodwill toward men. Yes, it was indeed a momentous time in the history of the world, the most momentous event of all times. It was the moment in time when heaven came down and kissed the earth.

Prepare yourself to take this imaginary journey by first carefully reading the account of the birth of Christ Jesus in the Bible (Luke, Chapter 2). Then prayerfully meditate upon God's Word about the first Christmas in Bethlehem. Pray that the Holy Spirit will guide your heart, mind, and soul to the time when Jesus was born so that you can be spiritually blessed. With the help of the Spirit, you will be able to visualize the glorious event of the birth of Jesus in a way that mere imagination is unable to visualize. After reading and meditating upon the first Christmas, let the Spirit of God open the eyes of your imagination. What do you see?

A World without the Spirit of Christmas

You are standing in the middle of the road that runs through the little town of Bethlehem. It is cold and dark; the night sky above glitters with a myriad of bright, shining stars. The road is congested with a heavy traffic of people. Most are walking while others are riding camels, donkeys, or horses. Almost everyone passing by have a dejected and a despondent look on their faces. On this first Christmas night, you know the reason for the late night travelers and where they are heading. Also, you know the reason for their travel-weary demeanor as well as the reason behind the look of deep despondency and hopelessness upon their faces. They are on their way to pay taxes to Rome. The tyranny and oppression of Rome are reflected in the demeanor and the faces of a people whose land is occupied by the world's greatest empire.

But, no doubt, later tonight the look of despondency and hopelessness on many of these faces will be changed to great joy and hope. Soon the shepherds will be spreading the good news throughout Bethlehem– the glad tidings of great joy that Christ the Savior is born. Indeed, soon the world for the first time will feel the Christmas spirit– heaven's gift of hope, peace, and goodwill. And the world will never be the same again.

But now, no one here seems to be feeling the Christmas spirit. There is no hope, no peace, and no good will. The oppressive power of Rome has taken its toll on a proud and independent people. Bearing the heavy yoke of a conquered people, these Jews must yield to the tyrannical power of the Roman Empire. They are now being forced by the imperial masters of the ancient world to travel to the region of their ancestral home in Israel. Many of these travelers are now converging on Jerusalem, where they must register for the taking of a census in order to be taxed, due to the decree from Caesar Augustus, mandating that the entire world should be taxed. Indeed, for these people, Caesar, like Satan the great wolf, comes only to steal, kill, and to destroy. But tonight, there will come another to restore, to heal, and to give life. He is the Messiah, the Savior of the world. And he will give to everyone the spirit of Christmas, the spirit of hope, peace, and goodwill.

The Divine GPS

Based on your knowledge about the event of this time, you know that it is due to the decree of the Roman emperor, Augustus, that Mary and Joseph have been traveling on this road to the little town of Bethlehem– the ancestral home of both Mary and Joseph. But suddenly you realize that this road is not exactly where you want to be. Where is the manger? You are not sure where to go next.

You now feel unsure and a little anxious about what will happen next. You are in a quandary as to where to go. Your present predicament is a little puzzling to you and underscores the possibility that you are not in complete control of your imaginary journey that is guided by the biblical account of the birth of Jesus. You are not exactly where you expected your imagination to take you at this time. Nevertheless, the feeling that you are being divinely guided is quite thrilling and most reassuring. Apparently, for some unknown reason, the time machine of your mind has transported you to the time of the birth of Jesus in Bethlehem, but not to the exact location of his birth, which is not provided by the biblical account. Instead, you are here on the road leading through Bethlehem, viewing a world without the spirit of Christmas. Nevertheless, you feel confident that the GPS guiding your mental time machine is about to "recalculate."

You wonder if the inn, where Mary and Joseph would have stopped to inquire about the availability of a room, is farther ahead down the road or behind you. Suddenly, you hear the bleating of sheep. Looking over the embankment of the road, you see white forms in the darkness. The white forms of sheep are conspicuous in the darkness of the night, but the dark shadowy forms of the shepherds in the distance can barely be seen in the darkness. You can hardly see them as they lead their flock across an extremely large field. Mental recalculation! Now you know where to go. You breathe a sigh of relief with the sight of shepherds leading their sheep in the field at night. The shepherds of Bethlehem, whom the Bible reveals were guided by the angels to the Christ child, will lead you to the manger of Jesus, and to the holy family.

Deciding to follow the shepherds, you climb over the embankment of the road, then walking briskly, you hurry across the dark, grassy field, where you eventually overtake them. You follow them across the wide open field, up a steep hillside, and then down into a deep valley. Reaching down into the lowest part of the valley, you watch as the shepherds herd the sheep together where they will be bedded for the night.

After herding together the flock of sheep, each shepherd positions himself on the grassy slope overlooking the sheep. Seated on the grass, they watch over them, guarding the sheep from wild beasts as well as thieves that roam the area around Bethlehem. Watching the shepherds guarding the sheep, you are reminded that Jesus, the Good Shepherd, is watching over you even now.

The Ultimate Time Change

Seating yourself on the grassy slope a short distance above the shepherds, you turn your eyes upward toward heaven. You look up at the night sky above with mounting excitement. However, the shepherds are occupying themselves with the mundane task of watching the sheep in the valley below. Little do they know about the extraordinary and spectacular event, which is about to change time forever. And is about to forever change their lives and the lives of countless millions forever.

Seeing the night sky filled with shining stars glittering in the blackness of space gives rise to the thought of the glorious light of heaven that will appear at any moment. Soon the heavenly light of the first Christmas will be shining in the darkness of the world, and "the darkness will not comprehend it." You feel your heart throbbing with the thought of the coming event. Emmanuel will come- God with us- the infinite will dwell with the finite, the eternal God will enter time, and the omnipotent God will take the form of Mary's baby. Amazing grace has found a way to a sinful world. And the world will never be the same again. Oh what a blessed thought! Tonight heaven will come down to kiss the earth.

Indeed, after this night the world will never be the same again, because a fundamental change is about to take place. This momentous event that is about to happen will not only divide time- dividing the time BC (before Christ) from the time AD (in the year of our Lord)- but this event will also divide mankind, separating believers from unbelievers, and the saved from the lost. However, if the event of his first coming divides time and divides humanity, it unites in the most wonderful way. Believers are forever united to God as their heavenly Father, and also they are forever united to each other as members of the family of God. And nothing will ever again separate true believers— those who are truly born again- from the presence of God.

As you reflect on the security you have in Christ, this verse in Romans 3:35 comes to your mind: "What shall separate us from Christ? Shall tribulation or distress, or persecution, or famine or nakedness, or peril, or sword? For I am persuaded that neither death, nor life, nor angels, nor principalities, nor powers, nor things present, nor things to come, nor height, nor depth, nor any other creature shall be able to separate us from the love of God, which is in Christ Jesus our Lord." Before the coming of Christ, you were separated from God by sin, but now never again will you be ever separated from God, because in Christ, God has become for us, "Abba," Father. Indeed, the Bible says, "Now, are we the children of God." No more are we just creatures of God, but children. How could this be? The amazing grace of God! The Good Shepherd gave his life for God's chosen people of every race and every nation throughout the world. They are the sheep of his pasture.

The Least Shall Be the Greatest

While seated on the grassy slope above the shepherds, waiting for the angelic visitation, you begin to take a closer look on the lowly shepherds, the world's first evangelists, called by God to announce the birth of Jesus. These humble souls, destitute of land and earthly possessions, are the chosen ones to proclaim to the people of Bethlehem the greatest news of all times– the news about the coming of Israel's Messiah, Jesus, the Savior of the world. As a sudden gust of cold wind starts blowing, the shepherds wrap their loose-fitting clothing tightly around themselves. Their shabby-looking and worn-out clothing is drawn snugly around their shoulders in order to warm themselves in the cold. Beside them is laid the tool of their trade, a shepherd staff, long and curved at one end.

While others in Bethlehem are sleeping in their warm beds, these poor souls, exposed to the cold and the night dew, must spend a sleepless night watching these sheep soon to be slaughtered, their blood shed for the good of the people. All these sheep will be slaughtered in order to feed or clothe the people of Judea, or to be offered on the altar of sacrifice in the temple as a sin offering. Your mind turns to Jesus, the Lamb of God, whose birth is about to take place in the little town of Bethlehem. Someday Jesus, as the Lamb of God, will also be slaughtered, and his blood will be offered on the altar of sacrifice to take away all our sins.

It occurs to you that just as they are now watching over these sheep, in a little while these same shepherds will be in a sense watching over the Lamb of God, sent from heaven by God to be the ultimate offering for sin– sent by God to give his life as a ransom for many. The words of Isaiah reverberate deep within your soul as you cast your eyes down on the flock of sheep to be slaughtered: "He is brought as a lamb to the slaughter, and as a sheep before her shearers is dumb, so he opened not his mouth." You are beginning now to see with greater clarity the true meaning of the Christmas story. For God so loved the world that he gave the world the greatest gift on the first Christmas day: God gave to the world the Lamb of God.

The sound of the bleating of sheep and the sound of the cold wind rustling the leaves of the surrounding trees, coupled with the night sound of crickets chirping, would prove to be constant distractions and annoyances for anyone trying to sleep. However, the shepherds are not trying to sleep; they are trying to keep awake. Therefore, the cacophony of sounds serve to help keep the shepherds alert and awake as they watch over their flock by night. Again you are thinking about your Good Shepherd. God never sleeps. He is watching you now– watching you on this spiritual journey. Indeed, you are a sheep of his pasture, and he has given his life for you.

The sight of the shepherds shivering in the cold while others are warm, safe, and secured in their homes is for you a rude awakening to the plight of these poor, humble souls living at this time and in this place. Without land or possessions and lacking any education or social status, they are viewed by their fellow countrymen as the least among them. Suddenly, the words of Jesus about the poor now come to your mind. When he was asked by one of his disciples about who will be the greatest in the kingdom of God, Jesus replied, "He that is the least among you shall be the greatest. For the first shall be the last and the last shall be the first." Certainly, tonight's coming event is a case in point about how God views greatness. And so, as the least in Bethlehem, the shepherds shall prove to be the greatest among their countrymen. Tonight they will become like the angels of heaven, God's messengers, the heralds of good news–bearing glad tidings of great joy to the world. The greatest news of all times will be entrusted to these who are considered the least in Israel.

The Angelic Host

Suddenly, everything is strangely quiet. There is complete silence. It is as if every sound from the restless, bleating sheep is abruptly hushed into silence. They are motionless, appearing transfixed in their various positions, every movement suspended. With their necks stretched out awkwardly and head noticeably leaned to one side, they all seem to be listening intently. The sounds of the night seem to be eclipsed by the deep hush of silence; the chirping of the crickets is hushed, the wind is stilled, and there is no rustling of leaves to be heard. And you no longer feel the cold like before.

The strange, deep silence is riveting– the thunderous silence deafening. And it seems nothing and no one dares to break the silence. There is something incredibly unusual, supernatural, and holy about this instantaneous, soundless phenomenon. The awesome silence is like a transitional pause signaling a momentous change in creation– God, the everlasting Spirit, is putting on human flesh to dwell with us.

Then in the deep, holy silence of the night, when you are beginning to feel that even the movement of time has stopped, you see a most wonderful sight. Light, the color of amber, seems to appear out of nowhere. It covers the entire landscape of the valley, looking like a brightly illuminated mist or fog. One of the shepherds seated on the grassy slope below, stands up and points toward heaven. High above you can see a bright shining light, also the color of amber, descending toward the earth, and following in its wake a most wondrous sight– a host of shining angels. With awe and wonder, the shepherds gaze upon the heavenly sight, their upturned faces now glowing in the radiance of the heavenly light.

But as the direction of the heavenly procession begins to turn toward the shepherds down in the valley, they crouch down, trembling now– this time, not from the cold, but from sudden fear. Quaking with fear, they fall on their knees. They stretch their trembling hands toward heaven in fright; their eyes wide with fear while the descent of the angelic host, shining with a brilliant light, continue to move steadily downward to them. Descending to about five hundred feet above the shepherds, the downward movement of the angelic procession comes to a halt. With glittering wings outstretched, the angels, glowing with transcendent radiance, silently hover above the frightened shepherds for a long while.

Finally, one of the angels flies down to the grassy slope where the terrified shepherds are kneeling. They are completely overcome by the awesome sight of the angelic host. Hovering only a few feet above them, the sweet angelic voice-sounding like the sweetest music to your ears-breaks the deep silence of the night.

"Fear not, for behold I bring you good tidings of great joy, which shall be to all people. For unto you is born this day in the city of David, a Savior, which is Christ the Lord. And this shall be a sign unto you; ye shall find the babe wrapped in swaddling clothes, lying in a manger."

The angelic face of this heavenly being– radiant and reflecting a loving tenderness– and the sweet angelic voice seem to have a calming effect on the shepherds. They now appear to be trembling less than before. But still they remain kneeling, their faces expressing the awe and wonder of the supernatural encounter. As soon as the heavenly messenger delivers his message to the shepherds, with outstretched wings he ascends to the heavenly host hovering above.

Soon a heavenly chorus from the clarion voices of the angelic host, now hovering higher above the shepherds, can be heard singing praises to God– a heavenly sound so sweetly melodious, so divinely inspiring that it is utterly indescribable. With exquisite rapture, you hear the angelic host, the greatest choir in all creation, sing these wonderful words of praises to almighty God– over and over again:

"Glory to God in the highest, and on earth, peace, and good will toward men!"

While praising God, the host of shining angels light up the night sky. The sky over Bethlehem exploded with light like a spectacular firework. Some angels can be seen flying with lightning speed around the valley, leaving beautiful shining trails of light. Other angels soar high up into the clouds then soar down to the earth again, with bright glittering trails of light glistening in the wake of their flight. Then a multitude of shining angels all at once soaring high into the night sky, burst into the air high above with exceedingly bright glowing lights like a gigantic firework. You find the heavenly sight above you so wondrously breathtaking. Eyes have never seen, nor ears have ever heard such heavenly manifestations of praises to God.

As you watch the angels flying above Bethlehem and listen to their praises offered up to God, it occurs to you that you are witnessing the first Christmas celebration. Tonight heaven has come down to celebrate the birth of Christ with the least in Bethlehem, the lowly shepherds. For a long while you breathlessly watch the angelic host; completely mesmerized by the heavenly sight. Then finally, the host of angels soaring upward toward heaven while singing praises to God departs with the heavenly light trailing after them. The amber light trailing after them becoming smaller and smaller and the sound of their singing gradually diminishing. You continue to watch in awe and wonder, thrilled and enthralled beyond measure by the heavenly sight and sound. Soon the host of angels disappears from view. Again the sweet refrain of this thought enters your mind: Heaven came down tonight and kissed the earth!

Finding Jesus

There is now silence. The deep silence that ushered the coming of the angels has returned. In the wake of the angelic visitation all of nature still seems to be in a state of awe and wonder. Like the shepherds, you listen to the sound of silence; but not for long. Soon the night sounds return. Again, you hear the bleating of the sheep, the chirping of the crickets, and the sound of the wind rustling through the leaves of the trees; the cacophony of the night sounds in the fields of Bethlehem returning. Everything is as they were before—except the shepherds.

The shepherds' encounter with the angels has resulted in a visible transformation. It is as if they have been renewed, recharged, and revitalized. They are no longer men shaken with fear but men moved by faith. Their shouts of praise, cries of hosanna, and peals of laughter as they begin to worship God touch you deeply while watching them. Finally, you are seeing what worshipping God in spirit and in truth is all about. Down in the dark, cold valley, a revival breaks out. The sound of their revival meeting drowns out every other sound. Shouting praises to God, they dance and leap into the air with unbridled ecstasy.

You recall from your reading of the Acts of the Apostles that the disciples on the Day of Pentecost acted in the same way. According to the Bible, when the Holy Spirit descended from heaven upon them, their praises of God were so loud and exuberant that the people thought they were drunk with wine. It occurs to you that these shepherds will be witnessing to the people in Bethlehem about the birth of Christ, in the same way that the disciples will witness about his resurrection after the crucifixion.

At length, out of breath and sweating profusely, one of the shepherds says,

"Let us now go even unto Bethlehem, and see this thing which is come to pass, which the Lord hath made known unto us."

Before he finishes speaking, the other four shepherds are hastily leaving. Completely unmindful of the sheep that are bedded in the valley, they grab their shepherd's staffs lying on the ground, leaving their sheep, and begin to run toward Bethlehem to find baby Jesus, the Lamb of God. With mounting excitement, you follow them, running as fast as you can to catch up with them.

Running up the slope leading from the valley, you finally overtake them; you continue to run behind them as they cross again the wide open field. While running, you begin to wonder how far it is to the little town of Bethlehem. You also wonder how they will find the baby Jesus, since the exact place of his birth was not given by the angels. Reaching the end of the large field, you leap with the shepherds over an embankment to the road leading to the little town of Bethlehem. And you continue to run behind them on the narrow, winding road up a steep hill. The road is deserted at this time of the night; everyone is asleep.

Reaching the top of the hill- feeling tired and out of breath- you see lights, shining from the town of Bethlehem. Everyone begins to run down the hill toward the little town of Bethlehem. As the shepherds enter the town, they stop running and begin to walk, while you follow a little distance behind them. Almost every home is in darkness. Walking slowly and looking around, as if unsure where to go, the shepherds finally come to a stop.

You realize that they are completely clueless about where to go. But not for long; in the silence of the night, you hear the cry of a newborn infant.

The cry of the baby is getting the attention of the shepherd, just as the bleating of the sheep got your attention earlier when, like the shepherd, you did not know where to go. The sound of the cry is coming further down the road, a little past a large building situated close to the roadside. The shepherds start running again, and you follow in their wake.

Reaching the large, sprawling building, with light shining from some of its windows, you recognize it to be an inn– no doubt the inn where there was no room for Mary and Joseph to spend the night. Once again you hear the sound of the baby's cry. The sound seems to be coming from over the right side of the road, where there is a small field, partly enclosed by clusters of trees. There are no houses to be seen in the field, only a large stable. A dim light shines from the stable. The shepherds stop in front of the stable, listening to hear the cry of the baby. They stand hesitantly, looking at the stable, their faces marred with uncertainty. Then for the third time, the sound of an infant crying is heard. Suddenly, their uncertainty turns to resolve, and resolutely they now begin to move down the path toward the stable. You walk closely behind them, your heart throbbing with excitement.

As you approach the stable, you can see a light shining from its far end. The stable is quite large, its numerous stalls filled with different kinds of animals. Looking into the stalls as you walk alongside the exterior of the stable to its other end, you see horses, donkeys, camels, and oddly enough, even a few sheep. The animals are all lying down on the hay in their stalls, appearing to be sleeping. Finally reaching the far end of the building where the light is shining, you look inside the stable. And you see Mary and Joseph with baby Jesus.

Worshiping the Christ Child

Mary is tenderly holding the baby in her hands. He is wrapped in swaddling clothing– strips of cloth– just like the angel said he would be. She is seated on a blanket spread on the ground, while Joseph is kneeling down beside her. Their faces beam with obvious delight, but with no little surprise– a most pleasant surprise– at the sight of the shepherds standing at the entrance of the stable. Joseph beckons them to come in while Mary places her newborn baby in a manger– a feeding trough for the animals in the stable.

You fall down on your knees with the five shepherds, and you bow your head down to the ground to worship the Christ child. Then raising your head to look again on Jesus, you gaze with wonder upon the most awesome sight: the face of the mighty God in the form of a baby. In the flickering lamplight, the face of baby Jesus can clearly be seen. A beautiful bouncing baby boy smiles sweetly as he looks on you. Wonder of wonders! The everlasting God has wrapped himself in mortal flesh– Mary's baby.

With joy overflowing, you worship the Christ child, as the shepherds worship. They worship kneeling down with hands and head raised upward toward heaven, and then bowing down with hands and head touching the earth. Over and over again, reaching up toward heaven and bowing down touching the earth while uttering words of praises to God, they worship the new born baby, Jesus, the Messiah– the Savior of the world, the King of kings and the Lord of lords. These words of prophesy now flood your soul with unspeakable joy: "For unto us a child is born, unto us a son is given: and the government shall be upon his shoulder, and his name shall be called Wonderful, Counselor, The mighty God, The everlasting Father, The Prince of Peace." (Isaiah 9:6) Indeed, Christ Jesus is all that. And he is so much more! Down on your knees beside the shepherds, you now experience true worship– the only way to worship: With humility, with a heart broken and contrite, and with a heart overflowing with the deepest love and adoration, you worship God in spirit and in truth.

You feel utterly overcome with love and adoration for your Savior. You feel just like the little drummer boy: wishing you could do something right now; something for Jesus– anything to show the depths of your love for your Savior and Lord; for Mary's sweet little baby boy. He has sacrificed so much because he loves so much. He has come to the world to be born in this stable, to lie in this manger, and to die on the cross as the Lamb of God– all for you. What more could he do? Oh what boundless love!

The eyes of baby Jesus now seem to be focused on you as you look upon him. Jesus is looking directly on you. An overwhelming flood of the sweetest and the most sublime feeling of love washes over you. Then you hear yourself singing. You are singing almost without any volition on your part– effortlessly, like the act of smiling or laughing. With your heart filled with love and adoration, you begin to sing for baby Jesus.

Just like the story about the little drummer boy playing his best for Jesus, you now sing your best for him. As you look on his adorable, smiling face, you sing "Away in a Manger," "Silent Night," "Joy to the World," and "O Little Town of Bethlehem." The sweet, tender smile on the face of baby Jesus seems to get bigger and bigger with every song.

Now you can clearly see the purpose for your existence. "And for his pleasure you were created," (Rev. 4:11). The Lord finds pleasure in your worship. Indeed, you were created for worship. You have nothing to give except to give worship to the Almighty. And now you realize that true worship is the greatest gift– perhaps the only meaningful gift that anyone can give to the Lord.

Looking up at Mary and Joseph, you can see that they are also worshipping with the shepherds in their own way. Wonder and awe are reflected on their faces as they look upon the Christ child. And you feel like shouting out this question to the mother of Jesus: "Mary, do you really know who you are holding? Do you know that this new born baby you have delivered has come to deliver you? Do you know that the One you are holding is the One who is holding together all creation?" You wonder how much this young virgin girl really knows as the blessed mother of the Christ child. Suddenly, you are overcome with the wondrous implication of the virgin birth: God became Mary's son so that all believers could become sons and daughters of God. Indeed, this amazing truth about the virgin birth is truly the wonder of wonders!

Your heart, soul and mind brimming with the wonder of the first Christmas, and feeling like never before the glorious and awesome presence of God, you are fully convinced that this journey of the mind is more than just a mental journey. Indeed, it is another spiritual journey– a holy pilgrimage. With a heart overflowing with thanksgiving for a most inspiring and enlightening journey, and with your cup running over with the blessing of God's holy presence, you now feel ready to close the eyes of the mind, eclipsing the mental images of the past– the heavenly sights and sounds of the first Christmas. Now you close the eyes of the mind to focus on the present world around you. And in the twinkling of an eye, you find yourself back to the present time.

Lessons Learned in Odyssey

Baby Jesus laid in a manger– a feeding trough– is a sign of his purpose for coming to the world. Jesus came as the living bread from heaven to give us eternal life. Jesus says, "I am the living bread which came down from heaven. If any man eat of this bread, he shall live forever. And the bread that I shall give him is my flesh, which I shall give for the life of the world." (John 6:51) Jesus came so you could be fed with eternal life. How do we eat of the heavenly bread to receive eternal life? Simply by believing on Jesus as Savior and Lord. The Bible says that whosoever believes on Jesus "shall not perish, but have eternal life."

Another lesson learned from your spiritual odyssey is the way God chooses those whom he calls for ministry. He does not choose the proud and the haughty, but the meek and the humble. The angels did not take the news of Jesus birth to the leaders of the Jews or to the greatest of the Jews, but to the shepherds– the least among the Jews. In the sight of God, your greatness is measured by your humility before God and others.

The choosing of the Wise Men from the East by God is another manifestation of the way God chooses men for ministry, by rejecting the self-righteous. The star of Bethlehem was not revealed to the proud and self-righteous people of Judea, who ultimately rejected Jesus, but to men from Gentile nations, who had a hunger and thirst for God, whom the Jews considered to be uncircumcised heathens. Jesus says, "But many who are the greatest now will be the least important, and those that seem least important now will be the greatest. (Matthew 19:30)) Furthermore, the Bible declares, "But he gives more grace. Wherefore, God resists the proud, but gives grace unto the humble." (James 4:6)

Timely Visit to the Transfiguration: You Are There

The following is based on the biblical account of the Transfiguration. (Luke 9:28-36)

"Lord, it is good for us to be here. Let us make three tabernacles, one for thee, one for Moses and one for Elijah." (Luke 9:33)

Imagine you are there. You can go back in time to see and experience one of the most wondrously glorious events of all times: the transfiguration of Jesus Christ. Read the biblical account of this event, then let the power of your God-given imagination, guided by the biblical account of the transfiguration, transport you through time to this momentous event.

Begin your mental journey by prayerfully meditating on the Transfiguration. Open the eyes of your mind to see the past so many ages ago, and start to turn the pages of your imagination. With the speed of thought, in the twinkling of an eye, you are traveling more than two thousand years to the past to arrive on the Mount of Transfiguration. You are here! Mentally, you have left the present and now have just arrived into the past, in the year AD 32. The place of your arrival is the Mount of Transfiguration.

Your heart beats faster with anticipation as you look down with the eyes of your imagination from the top of the mountain. Your eyes take in the breathtaking view of a most beautiful landscape far below the mountain– a lush green ruffled blanket of rolling hills and wide valleys spreads out below. The white washed homes of a small village glisten in the distance under the bright noonday sun. These homes are connected by a winding dirt road that meanders around the rolling hills. The road continues through a densely wooded area to the foot of the Mount of Transfiguration. Looking far down below close to the foot of the mountain, you can see numerous white washed houses near to each other, and situated at regular intervals along the narrow road, like a string of pearls embedded in the green blanket of the beautiful landscape below.

Then looking upward you see a pillar of cloud gleaming brightly in the noonday sun. The cloud is suspended high above the mountain under a blue sky. Through a wide opening in the middle of the cloud, you can see the sun, shining at its zenith.

Standing on Holy Ground

You are gazing at the spectacular view from the top of the Mount of Transfiguration, when you hear the faint sound of someone talking. The sound seems to be coming from somewhere inside the dense foliage down the mountain slope. You shift your eyes to the brown path that leads up the steep mountainside to the grassy slope near the top of the mountain. A fairly tall man is striding up the path leading from the dense foliage. Following him is a much taller man, who is trailed by two other men who are noticeably shorter in stature. All are dressed in the traditional Jewish garb of the time.

As the four men veer from the path and head straight toward you, you suddenly feel conspicuous, out of place. You become conscious that you are standing on holy ground--the sacred site of the transfiguration. Shyly, you back away from the place where you're standing, then turning to walk a short distance away to a large tree. You lean your back against its massive trunk and watch the four men as they approach. They are breathing heavily, perspiring profusely from the arduous climb up the steep mountain slope in the heat of the day.

As they arrive at the location where you were standing, the one in the lead stops, looks around, and gesturing with his hands, he invites the others to sit and rest on the grassy slope. With the adoring response of little children to a loving father, they sit down with him, eyes fixed upon him, waiting expectantly.

From where you are standing, you can plainly see their faces. Your attention is drawn to the one whom you identify as Jesus, the only begotten Son of God. Like the three disciples around him, your eyes are now fixed on the one whose visit to planet Earth has had the greatest and most lasting influence on mankind than anyone who has lived before or since. His visit has changed forever the course of human history. His appearance, as well as his demeanor, is exactly what you have always imagined him to be. But now as you gaze upon his face, the indescribable tenderness in his eyes touches your heart.

What Manner of Love

Suddenly you are overcome with emotion. Your eyes burn and tears course down your cheeks. You are surprised at yourself– you did not expect to feel this kind of emotion. A feeling of guilt washes over you, followed by a profound sense of unworthiness. You gaze in awe and wonder on the one who loved you so much that he died for you.

He has borne every sin you have committed, every sin you will commit after this day.

Once again, you feel as if you are in a holy place with the all-seeing eye of God upon you. It crosses your mind that Jesus knows exactly what you are feeling at this moment. Your mental journey to this place and this time is really a journey of the heart; you are feeling the love of God like never before.

Jesus begins speaking to the three men, addressing them by name. Peter, the tallest of the group, and James and John, whom the Bible reveals to be brothers, listen to his words with keen interest. Jesus is not speaking in English, the language of your modern-day Bible, but in an unknown language. You do not understand what he is saying to the three men. It is evident that there is a limit to your imagination, as it should be. You fervently hope now that it is being divinely guided. On your mental journey you can only understand the spoken words of Jesus that are recorded in the Bible. Certainly this self-imposed limit to your imagination will prove to be a safeguard to any vain imagination that might creep into your mental journey. No doubt, the language that you now hear must be Aramaic, since that was the language spoken by the Jewish people during Jesus' time on earth.

The three men surrounding Jesus seem rapt with attention, like students listening to the instructions of an esteemed and beloved teacher. Peter, more animated than the others, interrupts at various times to ask a question or make a comment. The two brothers, James and John, listen quietly, completely absorbed in what they are hearing.

After speaking with his disciples for several minutes, Jesus pauses, looks up toward heaven, and begins to pray. Peter, James, and John bow their heads and close their eyes as he prays. When he is finished, he looks on each of the men with a tender smile. Then he speaks to them again. Suddenly their expressions change to bewilderment. With a resolute look on his face, their master rises to his feet and turns to walk up the slope to the very summit of the mountain a short distance away.

As he nears the top, he stops, turns around, and with his feet slightly set apart and hands outstretched on either side, he stands gazing steadfastly into heaven. He turns his head toward the pillar of cloud high above--the same cloud that you observed before, when you arrived on the mountain. And again he begins to pray.

The disciples watch as Jesus prays for a long while. Apparently expecting a long prayer vigil, they lie back and stretch themselves out on the ground, their heads pillowed on their hands. They seem to be drifting off into a midday nap.

Steadfastly looking on Jesus, while your back is pressed against the trunk of the tree, you slide down to sit on the grassy ground, making yourself as comfortable as possible. You wait in anticipation for the awesome spectacle of his transfiguration. Jesus remains standing above you on the mountain slope, praying with outstretched hands and with his face turning upward toward heaven.

Everything you have read about his life on the earth now begins to flood your mind. Two major events in the ministry of Jesus come to your mind: the beginning of his ministry, when he was baptized in the Jordan River by John the Baptist, and the end of his ministry, when he was crucified.

At his baptism, the Holy Spirit in the form of a dove descended upon him, and his Father's voice could be heard saying, "This is my beloved Son, in whom I am well pleased" (Matthew 3:17). But three years later at his crucifixion– as he hung from the cruel cross with his nail-pierced hands and feet bleeding profusely, his face dripping with blood from the crown of thorns that pierced his head, his body bludgeoned and torn from the horrific scourging– the Holy Spirit did not appear and his Father was silent. On the cross he cried out in great anguish, "My God, my God, why hast thou forsaken me?" (Matthew 27:46). God the Father, who was well pleased with his Son at his baptism, forsook Jesus on the cross at his crucifixion.

Why? Why was God silent? Why did he forsake his Son on the cross? You know the answer, but yet it is still so incomprehensible: Jesus became sin for us, and the holy Father had to turn away from his son. Once again your heart melts within you as you reflect on His divine love. God loved you so much, he sacrificed his only Son for you. And the Son loved you so much that he willingly gave his life on the cross for you. Oh, what manner of love! Indeed, God is love.

The Light of the World

The event of the transfiguration of Jesus has always puzzled you. His transfiguration is as nebulous as the pillar of cloud high above you, that is now veiling the bright sunlight. You now see the cloud beginning to descend from above, moving down slowly, casting a dark shadow on the mountain. His transfiguration, which took place a short time before his sacrificial death, has never been adequately explained; you are still in the dark, so to speak.

You have never fully understood its meaning. Why was Jesus changed to light? Why were Moses and Elijah brought to the mountain to see his transfiguration? Where did Moses and Elijah come from? These questions have never been answered to your satisfaction. So you whisper a prayer that during your mental journey, God's spirit of truth will bring more clarity to the amazing phenomenon of the transfiguration– an event that up to now you have viewed only "through a glass darkly."

As you observe the descending cloud, while you ponder the mystery and the wonder of the transfiguration, you turn your eyes upon Jesus. His head is still lifted up as he prays with-outstretched hands, but you are beginning to see a change in his appearance– an almost imperceptible change. This is not what you expected; you have never imagined it like this before. You anticipated an instant change. But slowly, gradually, Jesus appears to be enveloped in the warm, soft glow of a golden light– the kind that emanates from the rising or the setting sun. But it is high noon; there is no rising or setting sun at this time of day.

Then you look above and see the same change in the color of the cloud; the white cloud has changed to the color of the same warm glow of golden light. And it continues its descent. You wonder about the change. Is the change in the cloud producing the change in the appearance of Jesus? Or could the opposite be true? The change in the appearance of Jesus is causing the change in the appearance of the cloud. You feel the latter to be true.

Glancing over at the disciples, you see that their eyes are closed, as if they have fallen asleep. And suddenly it happens! An explosion of blinding light bursts from the figure of Jesus. The surrounding landscape is drenched with blinding light. Reflexively, your hands move to shield your eyes from the intense light. But after a few moments, you slowly remove your hands from your eyes to squint in the blinding light in order to witness what is taking place. The clothing of the Master appears dazzlingly white, glistening with brightness. His face now shines with the intensity of the noontime sun. You notice some movement in the corner of your eye and so you turn to see Peter leaping to his feet, soon followed by James and John. They seem utterly overcome with amazement. Like you, they are trying to see what is happening, but must shield their eyes from the exceedingly brilliant light.

The cloud, now shining with the brightness of Jesus, covers the mountain slope. You are so overcome by the holy presence of God that you begin to wonder: Is this just your imagination, or is it something more? Can imagination become reality? And almost immediately, the answer comes with astonishing clarity: Imagination becomes reality when God shows up. He is here now- you can almost touch him. You feel the presence of God around you in a palpable way. You are beginning to feel that this must be more than a figment of your imagination. If you feel drawn closer to God, then it is real- it is spiritual reality. No doubt it is guided and directed by the

Holy Spirit, because you are now experiencing an incredible connection to God. Indeed, you are now certain that you stand on holy ground, if not physically then certainly spiritually. You are overcome with an overwhelming feeling of holy reverence and adoration as the eyes of your imagination look upon the image of the transfigured Christ, shining in his transcending glory.

And now you are beginning to understand the meaning of the transfiguration as you begin to worship the glorified Christ with the three disciples. You can now see the remarkable phenomenon of the transfiguration through your new perspective of God's transcending glory. You realize for the first time what the transfiguration was all about. It was about removing the veil over the incarnate God to display his transcending glory, a glory manifested in shining light. Indeed, it was a tangible manifestation that Jesus is the Light of the World, the Light that shone in darkness and the darkness could not overcome the shining light of the Truth, the Way, and the Life.

Peter, James, and John are on their knees, bowing before the transcending glory of Jesus, the Light of the World. With their hands shielding their eyes from the intense light, they attempt to look upon Jesus but cannot– the light is so intense. You can see the reflection of the glory of Christ upon the disciples: Their faces radiate great amazement, awe and adoration as they worship the divine Son of God.

The Two Visitors

Then Jesus ceases praying. He seems to be quietly waiting, focusing now on the empty space beside him. Then suddenly, out of the thin air, two figures appear. The disciples, jolting with astonishment, gasp audibly, looking wide-eyed at the two visitors who appeared out of nowhere. The visitors also seem startled, as if they are totally unprepared for their sudden entrance– their faces etched with amazement and wonder. With their hands shielding their eyes from the intense light, the newcomers look upon Jesus and immediately fall to their knees before him. The same expression of awe and adoration that you saw on the faces of the disciples now frames the faces of the two new arrivals.

The two men are a study in contrast. One is tall; a commanding figure, with a flowing white beard. He carries a long staff in his hand. The other is shorter in stature and seems much younger, his beard just starting to grow. He wears a mantle that covers his small frame. As they bow down at the feet of Jesus, the Master places his hands upon their heads. It appears that he is speaking words of blessing over them. Though you do not understand the language Jesus is speaking, you hear two familiar names: Moses and Elijah. Then you hear Peter gasp when he hears the names of these two icons of history. The disciples look at each other in astonishment, visibly stunned by the revelation that Moses and Elijah, who lived several hundred years in the past, are presently in their midst at this time and place.

Now Jesus beckons Moses and Elijah to rise from their kneeling positions. The light radiating from his face is still intensely bright, but it seems that Moses and Elijah are now able to look into the blinding light of his face. As they rise to their feet, they are no longer squinting or shielding their eyes. Unlike you and the three disciples, it seems that their eyes are now unaffected by the intensity of the light. They now look steadfastly upon his face, their eyes wide with wonder and adoration, as though they are looking upon the face of God. You can see how intently they are listening to the words of Jesus while he talks to them.

Based on the biblical account of the transfiguration, you know that Jesus is now telling Moses and Elijah about his pending death on the cross in Jerusalem. He is revealing to them the great sacrifice he will make in order to redeem mankind from sin. No doubt, this gospel is being preached right then and there to the two greatest prophets in Israel: "For God so loved the world that He gave His only begotten Son, that whosoever believeth on Him should not perish, but have everlasting life." (John 3:16)

Apparently, Peter is so overcome by the incredible sight that he is no longer able to contain himself. To see in the flesh Israel's two greatest prophets who lived several hundred years ago is just too much for him. Not knowing what to say, he says something anyway. (Peter is like that.) He calls out in a loud but tremulous voice, "Master, it is good for us to be here, so let us make three tabernacles, one for thee, and one for Moses, and one for Elijah."

Just then a loud voice booms from the bright cloud. It is like deep rolling thunder: "This is my beloved Son, hear him." Everyone is visibly shaken, quaking with fear at the sound of the voice of God. Peter puts his hands on his head and shrinks back in fear. James and John fall to the ground, also covering their heads with their hands. But Moses and Elijah gaze into the dazzling cloud, listening intently to the awesome voice of thunder, with rapturous wonder and adoration reflected on their glowing faces.

You wonder: Was the voice of God from the cloud directed to Moses and Elijah, or to the disciples? The voice of God affirms that Jesus is indeed the Son of God? Surely, the disciples must have known already that Jesus was God's Son, because God, the Father had already declared at his baptism: "Behold my Son, in whom I am well pleased." Also, the disciples followed Jesus, because they believed Him to be the Messiah, the Son of God. It is becoming clear to you now that the voice of God was directed not so much to the disciples but to Moses and Elijah.

You came mentally to the time of the transfiguration seeking answers to this mysterious event; now it just might be that you have found the answer to this puzzling question: Why did God transport the two prophets from their time to the time of Jesus on the Mount of Transfiguration? If the voice of God were indeed directed to Moses and Elijah, then it seems that they would only be brought to the Mount of Transfiguration for the following reasons: to hear the voice of God confirming that Jesus is the Messiah, to witness the glory of Christ, and to hear the gospel from Jesus himself, the Son of God. But you now wonder about God's purpose. What would be God's purpose for transporting them to the time of Christ to hear from God that Jesus was his Son, to see the transcending glory of the Messiah, and to hear about his great sacrifice on the cross for the sins of the world?

Chosen as Witnesses

Suddenly you realize that just maybe Moses and Elijah were brought to the Mount of Transfiguration for the same purpose the disciples were brought here– to become witnesses for Christ. Certainly, receiving the declaration from God the Father that Jesus is the Son of God, witnessing the glory of the transfigured Christ, and hearing from Jesus about his pending death on the cross would prepare them to become his witnesses. Indeed, they would need no more preparation to become the two witnesses who will confront the Anti-Christ at the "end time." Many Bible scholars believe that Moses and Elijah are the two witnesses in the Book of Revelation. Also, is it possible that Elijah's visit to the Mount of Transfiguration is related to the Bible prophesy about his return to the Jews as a witness for the Lord at the "end time" in order to restore the Jewish people to God? You can only wonder.

You can only wonder as you wander through the wonderland of your mind, guided by the GPS of God's Word. Indeed, you now feel the need to pray that your mind may be guarded from the temerity of a vain imagination by being overly speculative about matters that seem to be so nebulous to many theologians. You are now reminded of the truism: Fools rush in where angels fear to tread. The understanding of such mysteries in the Bible is quite nebulous and unclear, because the Bible reveals that in the spiritual realm you must necessarily "look through a glass darkly." Only the Holy Spirit can unveil such mysteries. Therefore, one must be circumspect in viewing spiritual matters.

As you muse on the mystery of the spiritual realm, you now find yourself completely enveloped in the brilliant white cloud. The intensely bright light in the cloud is so dazzling that it is as if your body has disappeared before your eyes; you can no longer see your hands, feet, or torso. You view with wonder and amazement your ethereal surrounding of shining light. Now the blinding light no longer affects your eyes– you can open your eyes without feeling any kind of discomfort. You feel at once a wonderful ecstasy, and a wondrously sweet solace. Suddenly, you are feeling refreshed and invigorated in the cloud that is swirling around you. It is like plunging into a refreshingly cool pool on a hot day. But there is really no way to fully describe the incredibly wonderful ecstasy you feel. It is beyond words!

The cloud engulfing you has become a heavenly pool of light, flooding you with unfathomable peace and serenity that touches the depths of your soul. The thunderous voice, which you just heard before from inside the cloud, now echoes through the canyons of your mind: "This is my beloved Son, hear him." Then you are struck by the thought: God is speaking personally to me also. As a time traveler of the mind– remembering the past– God is saying to you, "This is my beloved Son, hear him." You are also called to be a witness for Christ, your Savior and Lord. You have been chosen by God to tell your family, friends, and everyone who is seeking for God that Christ Jesus is the Light of the world, that he has died for them to redeem them from sin, and that he is the Son of God.

Basking in God's Presence

At this very moment, you are experiencing a marvelous spiritual encounter with God. You have an acute awareness of his holy presence around you, and in you, as you are enveloped in the pool of shining light. The wonderful presence of the Lord is now swirling around you like a whirlpool. The pool of light wraps around you like a blanket; it gives you a warm, comforting feeling, like you are being tenderly embraced in the loving arms of God. You are becoming increasingly conscious of the amazing love of God; he truly loves you with an indescribable love. Indeed, you now feel as if you are the apple of his eye– although so unworthy of his amazing love.

As you are immersed in the intense, dazzling light of the shining cloud, you can see now with exceeding clarity how Jesus's transfiguration is reminiscent of his baptism. For example, at his baptism, the Holy Spirit in the form of a white dove descended on Jesus, just like the white cloud is descending upon Him now, and also at his baptism the voice of God declared Jesus to be his Son, just like God is now at the transfiguration declaring Jesus to be his Son. Could it be that the Spirit of Truth is guiding you on this mental journey, revealing to you what you did not know before? In the baptism you now see the humanity of Jesus, who, as God, took on flesh to die for your sins. And in the transfiguration, you see so clearly the divinity of Jesus, who would be raised from the dead with transcending glory and power. Certainly, without the Spirit, there can be no spiritual understanding. Indeed, now you feel the presence of the Spirit all around you.

The Question of Time Travel

Now you notice that the shining cloud of light is gradually disappearing from around you. As the light fades, the day seems darkened, although it is still early in the afternoon. But then you realize that the day is as bright as ever; it is your eyes that are darkened. After gazing into the dazzling light radiating from Jesus and the cloud, it would take a while for your eyes to adjust to the normal light of day.

When the cloud finally disappears, you turn to look in the Master's direction. He stands alone now. Gone is the bright, dazzling light from his face and clothing. And gone are his two visitors, Moses and Elijah. His disciples rush over; they bow down on their knees before him in worship and adoration. Jesus raises them up, smiling cheerfully. They begin to talk excitedly to Jesus. But now you wonder, what has happened to Moses and Elijah? Where did they go?

And where had they come from? Your heart yearns for answers while you ponder these questions: Did they come from heaven? Are they heavenly beings? Spirits from the dead? A vision? But certainly, Jesus would not inform a mere vision about his pending death on the cross. And clearly, they are still mortals– not heavenly beings nor spirits from the dead. Peter saw this so vividly that he offered to make houses for them, because he obviously felt that they needed a place to stay. But how is it that they appeared on the Mount of Transfiguration as mortals, hundreds of years from the past? How can this be possible? Did they travel through time? You remember the core biblical truth:" With God all things are possible." There is no limit to the power of God.

However, you can never forget that your understanding of certain mysteries in the spiritual realm will be always limited. With your limited understanding, you must, therefore, walk by faith and not by sight or understanding. So, when you do not understand, and become perplexed, remember what the Bible says: "Now we see through a glass darkly, but then face to face, we shall know, even as we are known." In other words, the mysteries in this life shall only be known when you get to heaven. Thank God you don't get to heaven by the level of your knowledge about the spiritual realm, but you get to heaven only by God's grace through faith in the revealed Truth: Only faith in Jesus!

Moved with Compassion

As you look on the disciples, you can see how their faces express what you're feeling.

Amazement! Adoration! Awe! The Master's eyes are filled with loving tenderness as he talks to them. Then, slowly, he turns his head to where you are sitting and, for a fleeting moment, his eyes meet yours– lingering lovingly on you. Looking on you at that moment, he seems moved with compassion; the tenderness in his eyes floods your innermost being with indescribable peace.

And your heart melts within you again. The incredible tenderness and warmth of his unconditional love touches you to the depths of your soul; you feel a wondrous loving bond with your divine friend.

Then Jesus turns and begins to walk down the mountain slope, followed by the three disciples. Peter, James, and John walk silently behind Jesus, pensive and subdued. No doubt the transfiguration experience has left them in a state of profound wonder. You watch as Jesus and his disciples round a corner on the path and then disappear from view. You gaze longingly after him wishing that you could be with Jesus physically instead of only mentally. You wish you could at least physically touch the hem of his garment, like the woman with the issue of blood, who was healed simply by touching the hem of his garment.

Then you remember his eyes of compassion– the tender, loving eyes of God– and how at that moment for you, time stood still, when your eyes met his. Oh how deeply you were touched by his healing love! Yes, in that moment he touched you at the depths of your soul, and something happened; you now feel that in that instant, you were spiritually renewed by his healing love.

Indeed, you have not only been with him in your mind, but you have been with Jesus in the spirit: You came, you saw, and you worshipped! Certainly, on this mental journey back in time, the mystery of the transfiguration has been unveiled for you in a most remarkable way. You came seeking, and he found you. You came searching for answers, and the answer came to you. And more than ever, you realize now that it is not what you know that is really important; it is whom you know. And to know Jesus is to love him.

Now you are ready to return. For the return trip, you simply close the eyes of imagination. And in the twinkling of an eye, with the speed of thought, you are back to the present time.

You feel now like you are waking up from a dream, or like you have just seen a vision- the images from your mental journey still so vivid in your mind. The indelible image of the eyes of Jesus- filled with such compassion, looking so tenderly into the very depths of your soul- flashes in your mind once again. How you were so deeply touched at that moment! Indeed, it was his divine love- his unconditional love- that touched you to the depths of your soul.

Oh, the immeasurable depths of his love! How deeply moving it was to know at that moment how much Jesus loves you- despite the vile creature you are, living in this fallen world. Certainly, your mental journey has helped you to see more clearly this truth: it is not who you are that counts, but whose you are. God loves you so much that he paid the ultimate price for your sins with his own blood, and now you belong to him.

The awareness of the loving presence of God now overwhelms you with unspeakable joy. You suddenly realize that Jesus is right here now in his spirit, looking at you with the same eyes of compassion, although you can never be worthy of his love. He has promised never to leave you nor forsake you. He is only a heartbeat away, because you are, indeed, the apple of his eye.

Lessons Learned in Odyssey

The divinity of Jesus as the incarnate God was revealed, when the veil covering his transcending glory was removed. On the Mount of Transfiguration his divine glory was manifested in shining light. Indeed, it was a tangible manifestation that Jesus is the Son of God and the Light of the World. Jesus is the Light that shone in darkness and the darkness could not overcome the shining light of the Truth, the Way, and the Life. At the same time, the voice of God, the Father, declaring, "This is my beloved Son, hear ye him," also revealed to the disciples the true identity of Jesus, as the Son of God.

Jesus's transfiguration is reminiscent of his baptism, and reveals God's plan of salvation. For example, at his baptism, the Holy Spirit in the form of a white dove descended on Jesus, just like the white cloud descended upon him at his transfiguration. Also at his baptism the voice of God declared Jesus to be his Son, just like God at the transfiguration declared Jesus to be his Son. In the baptism we can see the humanity of Jesus, who, as God, took on flesh to die for our sins. And in the transfiguration, we see so clearly the divinity of Jesus, who was raised from the dead with transcending glory and power to give us eternal life.

Timely Visit to the Crucifixion: You Are There

The following is based on the account of the crucifixion found in John 19:16-37:

Then he delivered Jesus, therefore, unto them to be crucified. And they took Jesus and led Him away. (John 19:16)

For as often as you eat this bread and drink this cup, you do show the Lord's death until He comes. Do this in remembrance of me. (1Corinthians 11:26)

According to the scriptural account regarding the sacrament of communion, Jesus commanded believers to remember his death through the eyes of their imagination. We can see in the Scripture how he introduced the broken bread to remind us of his broken body– a body broken and bruised from a severe beating by Roman soldiers, with nails piercing his hands and feet and with a spear piercing his side. Jesus introduced also the cup of wine to remind us of his blood– streaming from hands, feet, side, and his bleeding head, pierced by the crown of thorns. Apparently the sacrament of communion is a means for believers not only to remember his death, but to also visualize his death on the cross.

Every time a believer takes communion, he or she enters the time machine of the mind to be mentally transported to the time of the crucifixion. As a result of such mental transportation, the death of Jesus becomes more meaningful to believers. Therefore, it is incumbent on every believer to always remember the death of Jesus, the Redeemer from sin, in the most vivid way.

So enter again the time machine of your mind to make a timely visit to the time of the crucifixion. Through the eyes of your imagination, you can witness the awful death of Jesus, when he died on the cross to pay the price for your sins over two thousand years ago.

Your mental journey back to the distant past to see the sacrifice of the Lamb of God will no doubt prove to be an unforgettable experience. Meditate on the account of the crucifixion that is given in the Bible, then prepare your heart and mind for a spiritual odyssey back to the distant past over two thousand years ago. Turn the eyes of your heart back in time to focus on the immeasurable love of God manifested at the time and place of your redemption. Now open the eyes of your imagination. In the twinkling of an eye, travel through time at the speed of thought to the time of Christ in the year AD 33. What do you see?

Behold the Lamb

The sight before you is revolting, repulsive, and so heartrending. It is utterly unbearable to look at the gruesome sight. On a hill, not too far away from where you are standing, you see three men hanging from tall wooden crosses. Your attention is drawn to the figure in the center, whose face is mutilated beyond recognition, his body covered with blood.

On his head, there is a crown of thorns from which a profusion of blood is flowing, saturating his hair, face, and beard. There is blood gushing from deep gashes on his body, his flesh torn with numerous stripes over his body. Streams of blood are pouring from his hands and feet, which are nailed to the cross. You cringe at the appalling sight of a Roman soldier thrusting a spear in his side from which blood and water is now flowing.

The sight is more than you can bear; you cover your eyes with your hands, unable to look on the ghastly scene. You are witnessing through the eyes of your imagination the most torturous death imaginable: The crucifixion of Jesus, who died as the Lamb of God over two thousand years ago. To see hanging from the cross the broken body of the Son of God, and to see his cleansing blood for all your sins, pouring from his body like a fountain, touch you beyond anything you have ever seen.

The sound of the jeering, mocking voices of hostile onlookers are all around you. Looking around, you find yourself standing in the midst of a throng of spectators, a short distance away from the scene of the crucifixion site. Several Roman soldiers are standing on the hill where the three crosses are erected; the hill called Calvary or Golgotha resembles the shape of a skull. You hear a mocking spectator behind you shouting, "He can save others, but can't save himself."

Another standing beside you also shouting, "If you are the Messiah, come down from the cross now. We're waiting! Come on!"

Then you hear his voice, and your heart melts within you at the sound of his voice as he cries out, "Father, forgive them, for they know not what they do."

How truly incredible! Jesus, God in the flesh, is interceding on behalf of those who have spat on him, mocked him, beaten him, and pierced his hands, feet, and side, causing his blood to gush from his body like a crimson fountain.

Traveling mentally to the time and place of the crucifixion is having an astonishing impact upon you. The words of Jesus forgiving his tormentors touch your innermost being; his divine love washes over you, and tears gush from you, like water from a broken pitcher. Who can forgive like this? Only Jesus, the Son of God, the Lamb of God, who came to die for you. At this moment his great love overwhelms you. Oh, the love of God!

The Love of God

You remember now the prophetic words of Isaiah written several hundred years before the coming of Christ. You marvel at the remarkable fulfillment of these words of prophesy:

"He was wounded for our transgressions, He was bruised for our iniquities, the chastisement of our peace was upon Him, and with His stripes we are healed...he is brought as a lamb to the slaughter." (Isaiah 53:5,7).

As you stand here facing the grim reality of the sacrificial death of the Messiah, there is suddenly a deeper understanding of the ultimate sacrifice of Christ for the human race. The reason why he came to our fallen world in the flesh seems so very clear. He came not to be served, not to be honored and adored by the world, but to suffer and to die for the sins of the world; Jesus was willing to suffer and to die because of his boundless love! His love so divine, so true, and so measureless could not be contained in heaven. For God so loved that he could never endure being separated from his people, the sheep of the Good Shepherd.

Yes, God so loved the world that he would endure instead the mocking, the pain, the humiliation, and the death on the cross. For God so loved the world that he gave his Son to be wounded for our transgressions, to be bruised for our iniquities. He so loved us that he gave his Son, that the chastisement of our peace would be upon him, and with his stripes we would be healed. Yes, God so loved sinners that he gave his Son to be brought as a lamb to the slaughter, to die on the cross, that whosoever believes in him should not perish but have everlasting life. Indeed, Christ bore the sins of the world, because he so loved us; and so now "Where abounded sin, grace did much more abound." (Romans 5:20)

While watching the suffering Messiah, who possesses the righteousness of God, dying for the sins of the world, the awful consequence of sin is becoming only too evident to you. Sin, which brought death into the world, has separated us from the holy God, the source of life. But Jesus is now covering our sins with his righteousness. He is laying down his life that is spotless, blameless, and without sin, to be a bridge of righteousness over all our sins. And now because Jesus has taken our sins and given us his righteousness, we can be reconnected and be restored to God, and nothing can ever separate us from the "love of God, which is in Christ Jesus," (Romans 8:38-39).

As you witness the crucifixion through the eyes of your imagination, you are seeing clearly for the first time how the torn fabric of the relationship between God and man was mended by God's divine love. It was mended by the scarlet thread of Jesus' life-giving blood. Jesus came to shed his blood as the sacrificial Lamb of God so that we could be washed and cleansed from sin; now we are forgiven. Everything now seems so crystal clear. You are experiencing a moment of transcending clarity with this marvelous revelation: God loves me so!

You wish the jeering, mocking crowd could see the bleeding, mutilated love of God hanging there on the cross. Indeed, the height and depth of God's love can only be measured by the cross. Oh that they would see like you are now seeing the great sacrifice of God's infinite love! If the scales of unbelief could only fall from their eyes, then they would see that Jesus is paying a debt he does not owe, simply because they owe a debt that they cannot pay. Jesus, the Lamb of God and the Savior from sin, is dying for the sins of the world:

"For God so loved the world that He gave His only begotten Son, that whosoever believeth on Him should not perish, but have everlasting life." (John 3:16)

If they could only see and feel as you are now seeing and feeling, then there would be no jeering and mocking but only worship and adoration and the deepest love for Christ. Indeed, they would love God with all their mind, heart, and soul, because as the moon reflects the light of the sun, so their hearts would reflect the marvelous love of God.

At the Foot of the Cross

Suddenly, you feel an overwhelming urge to go to him. You frantically push through the noisy, clamorous crowd, and begin running toward the hill, shaped like a skull. You race up the steep slope to the top of the hill, where the three crosses are erected. Then, rushing to the cross of Jesus, you fall on your knees, hugging the foot of the cross. You feel like this has happened before, that you have been here before. Everything here at the foot of the cross seems surreal. Here at the cross, there seems to be a confluence of imagination and reality; you feel incapable of separating one from the other. Time and time again, his Spirit has taken your sin-sick soul to the foot of this cross. The eyes of your imagination are now seeing the place, and the time where the Spirit has so often taken you as a desperate sinner in need of cleansing– repenting at the foot of the cross over and over again.

There is now silence around you, and the loud clamor of the crowd has suddenly stopped. You begin to feel a strange sense of exposure, as if you are being watched. However, you are mindful that no one can see you, because you are here only in your mind, or in your spirit, but certainly not in your body. This is only a mental journey through time. Then you are struck by this thought: God is a Spirit and he dwells in you. He knows your thoughts and your secret sins. You cannot go to Christ now in a meaningful way without first confessing your sins– all your sins– not only the sins of commission but the sins of omission: all the things that you have done, and all the things that you should have done, but failed to do.

Suddenly, you feel strangely self-conscious as you become increasingly conscious of your guilt and shame, your failure to repent from certain sins. With a heart broken with sorrow and remorse for all the sins of commission and omission, you look up to heaven, turning your eyes upon Jesus.

The face of the suffering Messiah is covered with blood, sweat, and tears. He has taken upon himself all your sins and the sins of every repented believer. As you look upon Jesus with a repentant heart, you are now being washed. You are cleansed from all your sins! Free from all your sins, delivered from guilt and shame, completely forgiven by God, you are experiencing at this moment the most perfect peace. There is healing love at the foot of the cross.

The silence is suddenly shattered by one of the two men, whom you identify as the two thieves crucified with Jesus. The man to the left of Jesus shouts at him, sneering contemptuously, "If you are the Messiah, save yourself and save us."

You cry out to him, "Only believe, and you will be saved!"

Of course he is completely oblivious to you. You are forgetting that he cannot hear or see you. It is becoming apparent to you that this confluence of imagination with reality is, no doubt, caused by the trauma of watching the suffering Lamb of God. You find yourself loving him now more than ever with all your heart.

Then you hear the other thief responding to him with a voice broken with deep emotion, "Don't you fear God? Don't you see that you are condemned? We deserve to be condemned, but this man has done nothing wrong." He then turns to Jesus, saying, "Lord, remember me when you come into your kingdom."

Again your heart melts within you as you hear the voice of Jesus saying, "Truly I say to you, today you will be with me in paradise."

Once more you feel overwhelmed by the love of God. With your arms wrapped around the foot of the cross, you cry out to Jesus, "Lord, my Lord, I love you! I love you truly with all my heart. You are my Lord and Savior, and my God."

Jesus slowly turns his head to look down toward the foot of the cross. And his eyes– tender with love– alighted upon you. There is a look of recognition in his eyes. Again, you are overcome with a strange sense of reality: everything seems so real as if you have experienced this event before. Your mind is now besieged with questions: Could I have been seen by Jesus over two thousand years in the past as he hung from the cross? Is it possible that while on the cross and with the mind of God, he saw me at Calvary, transported mentally back in time, embracing his cross on Calvary's hill? Did he see me with the infinite mind of God long before I was ever born– not in the physical dimension, but in the spiritual dimension? The look of recognition in his eyes is giving you the feeling– which defies logic and transcends human understanding– that while he was on the cross, you were in his mind.

Then slowly turning his head aside, his eyes now seem to be focused on someone standing behind you. Turning around, you see a middle-aged woman weeping, her face framed with exquisite agony. She is standing with three other women and a young man. The young man is standing beside the woman, supporting her with his hand around her shoulder. It appears that while you were standing at the foot of the cross they ascended Calvary's hill to get closer to the suffering Messiah.

The Tender, Loving Care of Jesus

Based on the biblical account of those who were present at the crucifixion, you instantly recognize the middle-aged woman to be his mother, Mary, and the young man to be John, the disciple whom the Bible reveals Jesus loved. Also present are Mary's sister and Mary, the wife of Cleophas, as well as Mary Magdalene. These disciples are all weeping; fear and despair are evident in their demeanor, and on their faces. They huddle together around the cross, like lost sheep without a shepherd.

Mary, the virgin mother of Jesus, looks upon her firstborn son with tears streaming down her face. When she sees the blood streaming down from Jesus hanging on the cross, she immediately collapses in the arms of John. The sound of her sobbing as John gently rocks her in his arms is heart-wrenching. As you watch the blessed mother of Jesus weeping so piteously, you thought about this prophesy of Simeon to Mary on the day Jesus was circumcised as a baby: "Yea a sword shall pierce through your own soul, also."

It seems quite clear to you that this prophesy has been fulfilled today. The spear that pierced through the side of Jesus has also pierced the soul of Mary. It would appear that the prophetic sword was raised against the Lamb of God from the moment John the Baptist proclaimed, "Behold the Lamb of God, who will take away the sins of the world."

Therefore, it is clear from the beginning of Jesus's ministry that he came not to reign as King of the Jews, who were predestined to reject their king, but to die as the Lamb of God for the sins of the world.

No doubt, in the mind of every spectator, Mary is cursed above all women as she stands at the foot of her son's cross, watching his tortuous death–certainly, not blessed above all women as the angel proclaimed. Revealing the blessings of Mary, the Bible says,

And the angel came in unto her and said, "Hail you that are highly favored, the Lord is with you, blessed are you among women." (Luke 1:28)

You wonder how Mary could be blessed when she had to endure such misery and suffering as the mother of Jesus.. How could she be called blessed when as a mother there was no place for her to have her baby? Jesus, who was born in a stable, had to be laid in a manger, a feeding trough for animals. How could she be called blessed when as a young mother she had to flee with Jesus to Egypt in order to save her son's life from King Herod? Indeed, how could the angel call her blessed when today a sword has pierced her heart? Then the answer suddenly comes to you as you recall the words of Jesus:

"Blessed are they that mourn for they shall be comforted. Blessed are they which are persecuted for righteousness sake for there is the kingdom of heaven. Blessed are you when men shall revile you and persecute you and say all manner of evil against you falsely for my sake. Rejoice and be exceeding glad for great is your reward in heaven." (Matthew 5:4-10)

Indeed, to believe in the Lamb of God as the Savior from sin, and to share in his suffering, is truly the greatest blessing. Mary, like every true

317

believer, is highly favored to be part of the family of God.

Looking down from his cross, Jesus sees Mary weeping. You see the expression of loving tenderness reflected in his eyes; despite his terrible agony on the cross, he seems moved with compassion for his mother. Apparently he is no longer mindful of his own pain on the cross; it seems that he is now only feeling Mary's terrible pain and anguish– the sword that has pierced the soul of his dear mother is at this moment piercing his soul with indescribable pain.

With tears coursing down her cheeks, Mary turns her head to look upon the Lord. Glancing on John, Jesus says to Mary, "Woman, behold thy son!"

Mary is steadfastly looking upon Jesus. But now it seems that she is not focusing on his mutilated face, or his pierced hands and feet; she is not even focusing on the blood streaming down from the piercing wounds on his body. Her eyes appear to be fastened only on the tenderness reflected in the eyes of Jesus; Mary appears deeply touched by the divine virtue and indescribable loving tenderness reflected in them. Almost immediately you can see a marvelous change in her. The eyes of Mary are no longer wild and desperate with fear and despair. Then she turns to look on John. She smiles affectionately on the son Jesus has just given her.

Jesus now looks down on John, and he says to him, "Behold thy mother!"

Like Mary, John appears to be no longer wild and desperate with fear, but he seems now to draw from Jesus the strength and virtue that is so evident and compelling, despite his great agony on the cross. Standing there at the foot of Jesus's cross, Mary and John hug each other in a loving and tender embrace while looking up on Jesus. The tender, loving care of Jesus at that moment touches you profoundly.

It occurs to you that at that moment in time the arms of John and Mary have become his hands, although nailed to the cross- His hands extended to hug and comfort them. And despite suffering unbearable pain, Jesus closes His eyes and smiles broadly, as if He is the one hugging and comforting Mary and John.

A Roman centurion standing several feet away seems to be paying close attention to the interaction between Jesus and the small group of disciples gathered at the foot of his cross. He slowly walks over in an uncharacteristically reverent manner for a soldier and gently beckons them to leave.

Turning their eyes to look upon Jesus one last time before leaving, they slowly begin to move away. But as they look into his eyes, the peace that only Jesus can give, the peace that passes all understanding seems to wash over them; no sign of fear and despair can now be seen in their demeanor and on their faces. You watch as the small group of disciples quickly makes their way down Calvary's hill and disappears into the crowd of spectators below.

It Is Finished

You kneel there for a long time, looking up with wonder and amazement at the awesome sight: God in the flesh dying for the sins of the world. He has taken upon himself every sin that you have ever done and every sin that you will ever do. And he will now die for you and go to hell for you to pay the awful price for your sins; for your sake he will possess the keys of hell and the grave to give you the greatest gift, the gift of eternal life– all for you. A savior is born, the angelic host announced at his birth. Oh, what a Savior! But now the horrendous thought: the giver of life, who became mortal, is about to die!

Then you feel the earth starting to shake. At the same time, everywhere is suddenly plunged into darkness. The cries, "Earthquake... Earthquake!" are heard everywhere. No doubt, everyone is now thinking that the sudden darkness and the shaking of the earth could be the harbingers of God's divine wrath upon them.

Everyone falls to the ground, quaking with fear, cringing with terror and guilt.

You cling to the foot of the cross, feeling the earth shaking under your feet. Then you remember the words of Jesus– his soothing, comforting words of mercy and grace: "For God sent not His Son into the world to condemn the world, but that the world through Him might be saved." (John 3:17).

You realize that what you are witnessing is not related to God's wrath, but it is all about his amazing love for the human race. The earthquake and darkness are not about divine judgement, or the rending of God's relationship with mankind, but it is about the mending of the relationship between God and the world.

The great wall of sin separating God from man is now tumbling down. The veil of the temple, separating the holy of holies, right now is being torn like the body of Christ. And now we have access to the Father through the Son. Through the sacrifice of Jesus, there is freedom from sin. Sin can no longer separate us from God. Praise the Lord! The dawning of a new day is now coming!

Suddenly, the shaking stops. You are no longer feeling the shaking of the earth, but the darkness still lingers. And now a long silence. No one is moving, no one is uttering a word. Then the voice of Jesus breaks the eerie silence. "Father, into your hands, I commend my spirit...it is finished."

At that moment the darkness vanishes. The light of day returns. The sudden explosion of brightness on your sight– the harsh glare of the sunlight after the pitch darkness– causes a burning sensation in your eyes. Squinting in the bright glare of the sun, you look around. Everyone can be seen prostrate on their bellies or bowed down on their knees. There is no more mocking and jeering from the crowd, their eyes looking wild with wonder and bewilderment. Everyone seems to be breathing a sigh of relief. But you find yourself almost wishing that today was judgment day for these mockers and tormentors.

Slowly and cautiously they begin to rise to their feet, but a few still remain cringing with fear. The words of the Scripture come to your mind: "There is coming a day, when every knee shall bow before Him" (Philippians 2:9).

You look upward to see Jesus, his eyes closed, head drooping, and body hanging limply on the cross. It is finished, indeed. The Lamb of God came to die for us. The work of redemption is complete.

Removing your arms from around the foot of the cross, where you have been standing hugging it, you notice how they are dripping red with blood; your hands washed in His blood, His blood that cleanses from sin. There is life in the blood of Jesus–eternal life. Oh the blood of Jesus that reaches down to this sinner!

You watch as the centurion approaches the cross of Jesus; there is a look of adoration and awe on his upturned face while he gazes on Jesus. He stops before the cross and stands there, unmoving for a long while, as if transfixed, while he gazes with great reverence at the body of Jesus. Then turning to the crowd, he says, "He is dead! The King of the Jews is dead! Truly, this was the Son of God!"

Kneeling there at the foot of the cross, your arms again embracing it, the thought enters your mind: you haven't seen anything yet. Sunday morning is coming! This scripture comes to your mind as you smile through your tears: "Weeping may endure for a night, but joy cometh in the morning." (Psalm 30:5)

Yes, Sunday morning is coming. The Son will rise on Sunday morning. And Christ Jesus will be risen, indeed! Oh yes, because Jesus paid the penalty for sin, it is truly finished.

So now, the time has come for the return trip; you close the eyes of imagination to return from your mental pilgrimage back to your time. And in the twinkling of an eye, you are back to the future, now into the present.

How real everything seemed to be on your timely visit to the past; your mental journey was like a vision. You look on your hands, which only moments ago were covered with blood– the precious blood of Jesus. And you now clasp both hands together to spend a sweet hour in prayer, your heart brimming with love and joy and thanksgiving.

You are experiencing once again how your mind, guided by the Word and the Spirit, can take you into another dimension– the dimension beyond the barriers of time and space. Indeed, as your mental journey to the past took you beyond the barriers of time and space, you found yourself entering another dimension– the spiritual dimension– to experience the presence of God. And here and now you are still experiencing the wonderful dimension of the Spirit where there is a sweet communion and a loving fellowship with God. He is here! Neither time nor space can separate you from God.

Lessons Learned in Odyssey

While Jesus was on the cross, you were on his mind. How is this possible? The Bible teaches that God, who is all knowing, knew you before you were born, even before the foundation of the earth. The Bible says that Christ Jesus is God in the flesh (John 1:1,14). Therefore he knew you throughout eternity– long before he created you, long before the earth or the universe was ever created. He knew you forever and he has loved you forever. So, because Christ Jesus, with the mind of God, knew you throughout eternity, while he was on the cross you were on his mind.

Another lesson from your spiritual odyssey is the lesson that the curse of sin has been reversed, because of the cross. The curse of sin is only too evident in the human race. Without faith in Christ Jesus, we must live our lives in quiet desperation– in hopelessness and despair. Sin, which brought death into the world, has separated us from holy God, the source of life. But Jesus has reverse the curse of sin by covering our sins with his righteousness. On the cross he laid down his life for us, taking our sins and giving us his righteousness, so we can be restored to God. Now nothing can ever separate us from the "love of God, which is in Christ Jesus," (Romans 8:38-39). The curse has been truly reversed, because in Christ death has been vanquished, and now we have been given life eternal.

Timely Visit to the Resurrection: You Are There

The following is based on the account of the Resurrection found in Luke 24:1-12

"Why seek you the living among the dead? He is not here , but is risen." (Luke 24:5-6)

It is time now to take another journey back to the past as a mental time traveler of the Bible. Hopefully, going back to the past will be another journey of discovery for you, and a time of spiritually exploring the mystery surrounding the resurrection of Christ. Once again you will be transported by the time machine of the mind with its unique capability to take you mentally back to the past. With the power of your imagination, you can see and experience in vivid details this momentous event of the past that is recorded in the Bible.

Experience again how your mind can become a virtual time machine to take you on a holy pilgrimage. Take a giant leap into the past, propelled by your imagination, and guided by the Word in obedience to the Lord's injunction to remember the events of your redemption: The Lord says, "Do this in remembrance of me." If you are truly led by the Holy Spirit, no doubt, you will witness through the mind's eye another awe-inspiring event of the Bible. Let the time machine of your mind take you now on a trip down the memory lane of the eyewitnesses to the resurrection. Read about the amazing event of the resurrection in Luke 24, as it was remembered by the disciples. Then meditate upon the resurrection of the crucified Christ as you prepare to go back in time

The incredible phenomenon of the resurrection is the wonder of wonders. Indeed, no other event can be compared to the Resurrection. Because of this unparalleled event, the human race was given access to eternal life. As you are meditating on the greatest event in the history of mankind (mankind redemption), your mind that has no barriers of time and space, will transport you to the year A.D. 33 and to the tomb of Jesus in the city of Jerusalem.

However, let me remind you again to be circumspect in your mental preparation for the journey to the past; you must allow your mind to be guided by the infallible word of God. If it is not guided by the GPS of God's word, you will experience a mere illusion and a perverted exercise in futility, produced by a vain imagination. Therefore, prayerfully meditate upon the Lord's resurrection. When your mind is completely enveloped in the reality of the word of God, and when it has the stamp of the Spirit of Truth, it will take you to the time and place that you are now meditating upon.

Now, just imagine. In the twinkling of an eye, traveling with the speed of thought through the dimension of time and the dimension of space, you have now arrived in the year A.D. 33 at Jerusalem–about an hour before the resurrection of Jesus. You are here in his tomb– out of your body, but in your mind: This is where you are now.

Entering the Tomb

It is dark and cold. There is a deep stillness around you. Only the sound of your breathing you now hear in the silence of the dark and cold tomb. Gradually, your eyes adjust to the darkness, and you now see dimly the faint outlines of a round, massive stone before the entrance of the tomb. Tiny specks of light can be seen filtering in through small cracks around the stone. The huge stone seals the entrance. Your awareness of the silence deepens with every passing moment. It is not the eerie or depressing silence of death, but a holy, reverent silence. It is a silence pregnant with life, like the silence of an unborn baby in the womb, silently waiting to be born– waiting to take the first breath of life, and waiting to break the silence with the cry of life. Soon there will be the triumphant cry of the angel: He is risen!

The rock that you find yourself sitting on feels rough and cold and quite uncomfortable. As you shift your weight to ease your discomfort, and feeling the cold and seeing the darkness, you are struck by the thought that tombs are made for the dead, not for the living; hence, your terrible discomfort. But then you are struck by another thought, a most awesome thought, which overwhelms and smothers your sense of uneasiness and discomfort. All your cares and fears are suddenly canceled out by this thought: Here is the place where death ends for us and eternal life begins. Indeed, you are now becoming acutely aware that this is the burial place for the "Seed," described in the Bible; the "Seed" that died in order to bring forth the first fruit of eternal life. You can hear the words of Jesus echoing in your mind with astonishing clarity:

"If a seed does not fall into the ground and die, it cannot bring forth life" (John 12:24).

As you meditate on these words, the image of the tree of life comes to your mind. The Bible reveals how inaccessible to mankind was the tree of life in the Garden of Eden– standing tall on holy ground where no man could go and bearing the fruits of eternal life, which no man could reach– until today.

The Tree of Life

Sitting in the dark tomb, you become immersed with thoughts about the tree of life and how it became inaccessible in the Garden of Eden to the human race after man ate of the forbidden fruit. However, unlike the tree of life, the tree of the knowledge of good and evil was made accessible to the human race. Although Adam was warned about the dire consequences of eating the forbidden fruit of this tree, he chose to eat from it and immediately died a spiritual death when he became separated from God through the sin of disobedience. His spiritual death led to his physical death as well as the death and decay of all of God's creation. Mankind's disobedience in choosing the tree of the knowledge of good and evil brought about the curse of death and destruction to the human race. Only access to the tree of life could reverse the curse from death to life.

The only solution to reverse the curse was eating from the tree of life. But it was beyond the reach of mankind, until today. Now the tree of life will be transplanted in our world; a world where death has ruled, where everyone is born to die–until the resurrection of the "Seed" who died in order to bring forth eternal life. Eternal life will be made accessible to all who believe in the promise of God. And the tomb of Christ, soon to be empty, is the place where the first fruit of eternal life will be manifested to a dying world; the dead seed in the tomb is about to spring forth with eternal life right here and now. Oh, what unspeakable joy! Jesus, the divine Son of God, who died to take away all our sins, will be resurrected now as the eternal tree of life today.

Sitting here in the tomb, you feel like you are about to explode with the incredible joy of the Lord. The words of the poet John Donne come to your mind: "Death you shall die." As you reflect on the inspired word of God, with the promise of eternal life through the forgiveness of sin, an incredible peace sweeps over you. And you feel covered with the warm blanket of God's divine love here in the dark, cold tomb, containing the body of Christ. This tomb will become like a life giving womb– a womb pregnant with the "Seed" of the tree of life.

Again, your mind is flooded with more thoughts about Jesus as the tree of life. The dark, cold, silent tomb, this place of death containing the crucified body of Christ, is producing a stream of thought; and this stream of thought is not about life ending in death, instead it is about death ending in life– everlasting life.

Oh what a blessed thought! Oh the glorious reality! The gift of eternal life will soon be given to everyone who believes. Just as mankind in his pride doubted God's words and in unbelief chose to eat the forbidden fruit, resulting in death, so now mankind can believe the good news of salvation and in obedience can choose to believe in Jesus, and live forever. The curse has been reversed! Because Jesus, "the Seed" died, eternal life- the tree of life- will spring forth, and this life will be given to everyone who believes in Jesus. The sweet sound of Jesus's words once again reverberates in your mind and heart:

"For God so loved the world that he gave his only begotten son that whosoever believes on him should not perish, but have everlasting life." (John 3:16)

In the dark and cold tomb, you have received this wonderful revelation: Christ Jesus, is the tree of life. Springing forth from the death of Jesus- the incorruptible seed- is the spiritual tree of life- soon to be accessible to everyone who believes. The true meaning of the resurrection is now coming to light and is incredibly clear in the darkness of Jesus's tomb. What is the true meaning of the resurrection of Christ that you are now seeing? That eating from the tree of life– that is believing in Jesus as the Savior from sin– leads to life, eternal life. God has reversed the curse of sin! Praise God forever more!

Standing on Holy Ground

Sitting inside the dark tomb, you peer through the darkness, trying to see the body of Jesus. But the dense darkness seems impenetrable to see through. However, after a while your eyes become more adjusted to the dark tomb, and you are now able to dimly see the interior. It seems to be a large hole, a dug-out cave of some sort, perhaps dug out of a rocky hillside. You continue to look around, but there is no sign of the body of Jesus. As your eyes are scanning the darkness of the tomb, you lean back to ease your discomfort, while you remain perched on a large, pointed-shaped rock. Leaning backward, you become conscious of something pressing hard against your back. You turn around, and there you see it– there on a bed of stone, the body of Jesus.

On the flat slab of stone on the edge of which you are leaning against, you see a long, white form now showing conspicuously in the darkness. It is laid on a bed of stone, which is carved out of the rock, protruding from the side of the cave. Slowly and cautiously sliding off from your seat on the pointed rock, you now stand over the form to get a better look. You look down with a feeling of tenderness and holy reverence on the body laid on the slab of stone. You see that the form is wrapped in a white burial shroud. Suddenly everything seems surreal and you become transfixed where you are standing with this awful realization: It is the Lord's body! You now have the feeling that you are standing on holy ground, and you dare not touch him or touch the place where he is laid. For a long moment you stand there, transfixed as if frozen in time, clasping your hands together in deep reverence. Feeling out of place, and feeling the urge to move from this holy place, you begin to quickly move away, groping your way through the darkness of the tomb, moving to the far side. Here you stand in the darkness, waiting. You wait for his rising, like one eagerly waits for the rising of the morning sun.

The Wonder of God's Amazing Love

While leaning on the jagged wall of the tomb, the thought of Jesus, coming to the world in order to die for you on the cross, whirls through your mind. The thought of his amazing love now floods your mind like the thought of the tree of life just moments ago.

He loved you so that he died for you. You remember his words: "Greater love than this hath no man that a man lay down his life for his friends" (John 15:13). The thought enters your mind that at this very moment he is thinking about you and he is thinking about every soul destined for eternal life. Because of his great love for you, he is now preparing to enter his body, lying here in the tomb, even as he entered Mary's womb when she discovered that life was within her.

The wonder of his coming to the earth is so exceedingly wondrous that you find this truth beyond comprehension: God became flesh in the womb of a virgin. Wow! God created himself in an earthly form– the form of the God-Man, immortality putting on mortality. Why? Because God so loved us. But another great wonder of his love comes to your mind– the new creation of mankind, mortality putting on immortality. Because of the glorious resurrection that is about to take place–when the Spirit of Jesus enters his dead body to live again in a transformed, glorified, immortal body– all believers, who are truly born again, someday will also experience the same supernatural transformation. Some day in the resurrection of all believers, like Jesus, your mortality will put on immortality. Praise the Lord! Every believer will live forever!

How wonderful, how truly marvelous is the love of Christ! Jesus, the first fruit of the resurrection and the embodiment of God's amazing grace to mankind, has become the precursor of your resurrection. His soothing, comforting words now enter your mind, refreshing your soul with hope that springs eternal: "He that believes on me, although he was dead, yet shall he live" (John 11:25).

Tears of the sweetest joy begin to flow with this most comforting thought: Because he lives, all fear of death is gone; we will rise again. Yes, we will rise again to live eternally! Again the good news of the gospel now floods your mind and soul: "For God so loved the world that He gave His only begotten son that whosoever believes on Him should not perish, but have everlasting life." (John 3:16)

Suddenly, you are overcome by the depths of God's love for you. Your face is now washed with a flood of tears– a fountain of joy overwhelms your soul. Here in the tomb of Jesus, as you wait to see his resurrection through the eyes of your imagination, you are beginning to get a glimpse of the incredible depths of God's amazing love. The wonder of God's amazing love is truly the wonder of wonders– far beyond human comprehension is the love of your creator, who has now become your redeemer.

Trying to wrap your mind around God's love, you think about the purest form of love that you have ever known– a mother's love for her child. As you think about a mother's love, so pure and so true, you realize that her love, although so wondrously strong and binding, nevertheless is only the merest infinitesimal reflection of God's infinite and eternal love. As the light of the moon pales beside the dazzling light of the sun, so the greatest human love in this world pales beside the amazing love of God.

Standing here in the tomb of Jesus, who gave his life on the cross that you could have eternal life, you are beginning to see more than ever before, with unbelievable clarity, the boundless love of God. Long before you were conceived in your mother's womb, you were conceived in the mind of God. You are struck by the thought that you have been in the mind of God infinitely longer than the nine months of your mother's pregnancy. Indeed, you realize now that God's mind was pregnant with you long before the world was ever created. The Bible teaches that every hair on your head is numbered by God. He knew the color of your eyes long before the sun or the moon and stars were ever created. He knew that you would take this mental journey to his tomb, and your response to his love, long before the creation of time and space.

It is becoming increasingly clear to you why God's love for you is so great. If God has known you infinitely longer than your loving mother or your dearest loved one, shouldn't his bond with you be infinitely stronger? Indeed, God's love is the only perfect love. Oh perfect love, so pure, so true! His divine love is touching you now as never before.

Wiping away the tears coursing down your cheek while you meditate on the love of God, and feeling his love as you have never felt it before, the words of the song "The Love of God" comes to your mind. While standing in the dark, cold tomb, waiting for the resurrection of Jesus, your voice breaks the silence of the tomb as you now sing this song with your heart overflowing with the deepest love for your creator and redeemer:

"The love of God is greater far than tongue and pen can ever tell. It goes beyond the highest star, and reaches to the lowest hell...Could we with ink the ocean fill, and were the sky of parchment made, were every stalk on earth a quill, and every man a scribe by trade; to write the love of God above would drain the ocean dry, nor could the scroll contain the whole, though stretched from sky to sky. O love of God, how rich and pure! How measureless and strong! It shall forever more endure the saints' and angels' song."

How truly indescribable is the love of your creator, who became a man in order to die and pay the penalty for your sins! And now he will raise himself from the dead so that you can have abundant life and live forever with him in heaven.

The Rising

In the darkness of the tomb, while you lean your back against the cold wall of the grave of Jesus, the thought about all the graves throughout the ages that contain the mountainous dust of mortality enters your mind. You think about the countless billions of souls that have died through the ages– souls that have perished without the knowledge of salvation through Christ Jesus.

The tragic fall of mankind brought death into the world; the precious breath of life that God breathed into every soul became corrupted with sin, which brought death to every living soul. Therefore, the Bible calls sin the sting of death. Although every soul clings onto existence in this world, clinging on for dear life, still life remains so fleeting, and the breath of life soon expires. Everyone has an expiration date; every soul is born to die. Yet every soul yearns to live. Indeed, how true it is that all men must live their lives in quiet desperation. They silently live in hopelessness, fear, and despair– all condemned to death.

But praise to God, his marvelous grace found a way- the way of God's amazing grace! The Father sent his Son to bring life to all who believes. The Bible says, "For the wages of sin is death, but the gift of God is eternal life" (Romans 6:23).

Without Christ, you and everyone are indeed born to die, but when you believe in him as the Savior from sin, you are born again to new life-everlasting life. Yes, millions of believers will rise from their graves upon the return of Christ. God has given this promise to every believer:

"For the Lord himself shall descend from heaven with a shout., with the voice of the archangel , and with the trump of God, and the dead in Christ shall rise first. Then we which are alive and remain shall be caught up together with them in the clouds, to meet the Lord in the air, and so shall we ever be with the Lord." (1 Thessalonians 4:16-17)

This tomb of Jesus, which soon will be empty, is the reason for the happy ending to the life story of every believer. As a result of his resurrection, every believer can shout triumphantly, "Because he lives all fear of death is gone!" After the tragic fall, there will be a glorious rising.

Leaning against the side of the tomb– this small, dug-out hole in the side of a mountain– you wait for the inevitable, anticipating with mounting excitement the moment when the Spirit of life returns to the body of Jesus. But how it will happen, you do not really know. Actually, you have never imagined how his resurrection might be before. But increasingly, you are realizing that what you are experiencing at this moment could be far more than just mere imagination at play here. Indeed, if the Spirit is truly in control, then you could be impacted by this experience in ways that you could never imagine.

In the dark, cold tomb, you wait and wait, wondering how the resurrection of Jesus will unfold through the eyes of your imagination. Now suddenly, something seems to be happening.

The white sheet or shroud over the body of Jesus now appears to you to be whiter than before.

Watching intently for a while, you can see that there is a glow emanating from underneath the white shroud. The body of Jesus is gradually glowing brighter and brighter moment by moment. Soon his body is shining exceedingly bright and the shroud over his body appears to be translucent.

Suddenly it happens! There is an explosion of shining light; the blinding light is shining with the intensity of the noon day sun. Inside the tomb is now exceedingly bright. The walls of the tomb are shining dazzlingly white with the intense, bright light.

You close your eyes against the blinding light, but under your closed eyelids you see the redness of blood; such is the intensity of the light that it seems to penetrate your closed eyelids. You cover your eyes with your hands as a shield against the brightness. You wonder how the disciples coped when they saw such a vision of blinding light upon the Mount of Transfiguration, when the light from his face was as bright as the sun.

Then you feel the ground beneath you shake, and you hear the sound of a loud rumble at the entrance of the tomb. You don't know what is happening. Is it an earthquake? Or is the shaking from the stone being rolled away? Finally, the shaking stops. Cautiously, you remove your hands covering your eyes, but with eyes still closed. Under your tightly closed eyelids, you see now only the normal grayish black; the blinding light is gone. You open your eyes. And you see Jesus.

Standing before the open entrance of the tomb, he is looking at you with a tender smile on his face. Reaching out both hands toward you, as if to welcome you, he looks on you with eyes of deep compassion. He is clothed in a shining white garment. His face is suffused with the most tender, the most caring and the most loving expression that could ever be imagined by anyone. You feel an indescribable peace and a sweet serenity that reaches to the depths of your soul. You gaze in wonder upon the awesome presence of the risen Christ. Then you notice the nail prints in his hands as he reaches out to you. And you feel your heart melting within you.

Bowing your head in humble adoration, you fall on your knees before him. As you kneel down at his feet, you see the nail prints caused by the nails that pierced his feet to the cross. Yes, now you can see even more clearly the awesome truth of his divine love, as you kneel there before your God and as you feel your heart overflowing with love for him. Truly, his love for you is from everlasting to everlasting. Indeed, it is so true: While he was on the cross, and when he arose from the grave– long before you were ever born– you were in his mind. Yes, it is really true: God has forever carried you in his mind, because you have forever lived in his heart.

He has always known you, and he knew that you would be guided by his Word to take this mental journey to this time and this place in remembrance of his resurrection. It is no accident that you are here now– not in body but in mind and spirit. The divine love of your Lord and Savior has drawn you to this time and place.

As you remain kneeling before the risen Christ, you wonder, Where does imagination end and reality begin? Your imaginary journey has become so surreal. You know that in the spiritual realm, what you are now imagining is really taking place at this very moment. Jesus, who has promised never to leave you nor forsake you, is indeed standing over you, with his nail-pierced hands stretched out, blessing you. This is now happening in the invisible world of the spiritual realm. You are the apple of his eye, and he is actually looking down on you right now, with his heart filled with love and compassion. Indeed, what you are imagining is actually happening in the spiritual realm.

You lift up your head to look at the face of Jesus once again with a thankful heart for the amazing love of God. But he is gone. You look around, but you see only the empty tomb. You realize that with the eyes of your imagination you are no longer seeing Jesus here in the tomb, but in your spirit you know that he is here within you; his image is gone from your mind's eye– the imagination– but his Spirit remains in your heart and soul. You no longer need to imagine being in his presence, because you can feel his presence now; it is all around you. The presence of the Lord is now so palpable to you– so very real. Indeed, your journey of the mind has become a journey of the heart– a spiritual journey.

He Is Risen Indeed

You walk through the entrance of the tomb into the morning sunlight. Turning your face toward the east, you are greeted by the most glorious sunrise. The spectacular sunrise is utterly breathtaking. Moving farther down the hill away from the tomb, you find a place to stand, where the view of the sunrise is unobstructed by the trees close to the tomb of Jesus.

In the subdued light of early morning, the clouds are ablaze with colors of fiery red and flaming yellow, with gloriously stunning shades of shimmering purple and radiant with colors of pink and amber– the same kind of sunrise and sunset you sometime see on other timely visits to the past. Looking on the spectacular beauty of the sunrise, you wonder if you are getting a glimpse of what heaven looks like. But you know only too well that looking on this glorious sunrise with your limited imagination is like looking "through a glass darkly" on heaven's transcending beauty, a beauty that is beyond the imagination because it is so incomparable.

And you also know only too well that no matter how transcending the beauty of heaven will be, certainly for every believer, it cannot be compared to the beauty of the risen Lord, who sacrificed his life for your sin and conquered death and hell, so you can live with him forever in heaven..

Looking on the beautiful sunrise, you feel homesick for heaven, where Jesus has gone to prepare a place for believers. How wondrously marvelous to know that someday the grave of every believer will be empty, and we shall rise to our eternal home beyond the sky.

Turning around to look back at the empty tomb, you are suddenly startled at the unexpected sight. A man with a countenance like lightening and clothes white as snow is seen sitting on the stone that was rolled away from the entrance of the tomb.

At once you realize that he must be the angel of the Lord who rolled away the stone. The angel is not looking in your direction but looking down the other side of the hill, where two figures can be seen in the distance, climbing up the hill toward the tomb. As they climb the hill, getting closer to where you are standing, you can see that they are two women, both dressed in black. Based on the biblical account of Jesus's resurrection, you are able to identify them as Mary Magdalene and the other

Mary. They are walking up the hill, not looking ahead, but looking down on the ground while they talk together. The angel is sitting erectly on the stone while he watches with apparent keen interest the two women as they approach.

Nearing the entrance of the tomb, one of the women looks up. Seeing the angel, she gasps with fright. The other woman, also looking up, shrieks out loudly; both appear terribly frightened at the sight of the angel, whose countenance is shining with an intense light with the brightness of lightening.

Calmly getting up from where he was seated on the stone, the angel walks toward them while both women are frantically clinging to each other. The angel says, "Don't be afraid. I know that you are seeking Jesus, who was crucified. He is not here, because He is risen, as He said He would be! Come; see the place where the Lord was laying."

The faces of Mary Magdalene and the other Mary are livid with fear. You follow them as they follow the angel into the tomb. Still clinging onto each other for support, and trembling with fear, they look down on the slab of stone where the body of Jesus rested. They see lying on the stone the Lord's linen burial clothes and the napkin that was about his head. The napkin is not lying with the linen clothes, but it is wrapped together in a place by itself. A look of wonder and amazement is reflected on their faces. No longer trembling with fear and clinging onto each other, their hands are now lifted and their faces are now turned upward toward heaven in an attitude of praising and worshiping God.

You hear the angel saying to them, "Go quickly and tell his disciples that he is risen from the dead. Behold He goes before you into Galilee; there shall you see Him: Lo, I have told you!"

In reverent obedience, Mary Magdalene and the other Mary hurriedly make their way out of the tomb. You watch them as they begin to run down the hill, waving their hands toward heaven, wild with wonder and bursting with unspeakable joy. And as you watch them running down the hill, the same wonder and the same unspeakable joy like a flood wash over you, and you hear yourself crying out from the depths of your soul, "He is risen, Jesus is risen, indeed! O death, where is thy sting? O grave, where is thy victory? Death you shall die. He lives! he lives! Christ is alive!"

You turn to look toward the empty tomb. But there is no sign of the angel. He is gone; mission accomplished. The mission of the angelic messenger of God was to deliver the message that Jesus is risen. Suddenly, you realize that you have the same mission. It is the mission of every believer to tell the world that Jesus lives. You can hear the still, small voice of the Spirit speaking to your heart even now: "Go tell this good news on the mountain and in the valley, tell it on the highways and the byways, tell it to your church and at your job, in your home and in your neighborhood, tell everyone that the tree of life has been transplanted to our fallen world– tell the world that Jesus is risen. He lives!"

Realizing that it is now time to go back to the future, you close the eyes of your imagination. And in the twinkling of an eye, with the speed of thought, you are carried back to the present time.

Hear and now you are feeling the presence of God to be just as palpable and just as real as when you were mentally transported to the resurrection. Again, you feel the same holy presence with you. In your spirit you can sense his presence; there is the sweet awareness that he is still standing over you even now. With great compassion, he is still tenderly reaching down with his nail- pierced hands to bless you. Indeed, there is no doubt in your mind about the true meaning of your trip back in time: You are convinced that your imaginary journey back in time was truly a spiritual journey– a holy pilgrimage

Feeling wondrously inspired and renewed by the awesome spiritual encounter with the resurrected Christ, you begin to thank God. Indeed, you have been profoundly impacted by your imaginary journey, which has become essentially a spiritual journey. It is clear to you that what you are now experiencing is far more than just a figment of the imagination. You feel certain that the Spirit of God has given substance and meaning to your mental journey as evidenced by the enhanced spiritual awareness that you are experiencing right now. Indeed, on your spiritual odyssey, important lessons have been learned.

Lessons Learned in Odyssey

Christ Jesus represents the tree of life that has been transplanted to our dying world. Mankind in disobedience to God chose to eat the forbidden fruit from the tree of knowledge of good and evil, which resulted in death. From that time mankind had no access to the tree of life. But now mankind has access to the transplanted tree of life. We can now choose to eat from the transplanted tree of life and live forever, simply by believing in the resurrected Jesus. The Bible says, "Jesus is the way, the truth and the life." The curse of death has been reversed by the gift of eternal life.

Another lesson from your spiritual odyssey is that as a believer, you are a messenger of God. You have the same mission as the angel, who announced to the disciples that Jesus is risen. You have been sent by God to the world with the message of the gospel that Jesus is risen, that he has conquered death, hell and grave, and that he is now Savior and Lord. Now you need to pray that God will give you the boldness to witness to everyone, starting with your family and friends.

Timely Visit to the Rapture: You Are There

The following is based on the account of the Rapture found in 1 Thessalonians 4:13-18

"The dead in Christ shall rise first... then we who are alive and remain shall be caught up together with them in the clouds to meet the Lord in the air." (1Thessalonians 4:16-1 7)

The prophetic word of God reveals certain future events that will impact the lives of believers. Prophets of God, looking down the corridors of time through the telescopic lens of the Holy Spirit, have seen with incredible clarity events thousands of years in the future. A review of history reveals that most Bible prophesies have already been fulfilled or have come to pass.

One of the biblical prophesies that remains to be fulfilled is the Rapture. The Bible reveals that the second coming of Christ will be preceded by the event of the rapture, which is the "catching away" of Christians from the world. According to Bible prophesy, this heart-throbbing, mind-boggling event that all true believers are waiting and yearning to see will take place in the very near future.

After reading about the prophetic account of the rapture in the Bible (1 Thessalonians 4:13-18), turn the pages of your imagination to visualize this incredibly wondrous event. If you let your imagination be guided by the Word and the Spirit, it will take you to the not-too-distant future. Up to now you have traveled mentally to biblical events in the past, but now you can be a mental traveler to a future event, which undoubtedly is the most mind bending event of all times. It is certainly possible that you could be alive during the time of the Rapture, so you could be traveling mentally to your future.

If you happen to die before the time of the Rapture, then you will be resurrected from the dead just before you are caught up to heaven. However, the Bible reveals that if you are alive at that time as a believer in Christ, you will be caught up with other living believers to meet Jesus in the clouds upon his return to take all believers to heaven. It is most comforting to know that as a born again believer whether dead or alive you will be caught up to meet Jesus.

Let the time machine of your mind take you to the time of the Rapture. Now, visualize this event that could take place at any moment. According to the Bible, we are approaching the latter part of the "end time," and soon you could hear the trumpet of God sounding and see the dead in Christ rising first to meet Jesus, and you could be caught up with living believers to meet Jesus in the air.

Perhaps, reading about the rapture and imagining what it will be like is one way to be prepared for this momentous event that could come at any moment. The Bible warns, "But about that day and hour, no one knows." (Mark 13:32)

Pray that the Lord will guide your imagination as you meditate on the prophetic word of God. Let his word become a spiritual lamp to enlighten your mind and a spiritual path to guide your imagination. Meditate on the Word as you imagine the Rapture. Now, open the eyes of your imagination to travel mentally to your future as a believer. What do you see?

The Man in the Clouds

You are standing at your bedroom window, gazing on a breathtakingly beautiful sight- a sight you have often seen but now the sight is far more breathtakingly beautiful. You are looking on what appears to be a wondrously glorious sunrise. Minutes before you were awakened by the sound of someone shouting and a loud noise- like a trumpet sound. You are now thinking that you must have been in a deep sleep, because the night seemed to have gone by so quickly. You are now watching the glorious sight of clouds ablaze with colors of fiery red and flaming yellow, with stunning shimmering shades of purple and radiant with pink and amber. Standing transfixed at the window, you are utterly enthralled by the sight of the heavenly beauty of a most spectacularly beautiful sunrise. The heavenly beauty of the clouds in vibrant, gleaming colors touches your innermost being, giving you a feeling of sublime peace and a sweet serenity.

Looking out the window, your eyes become fastened on this spectacular view of shimmering light in radiant colors. The shimmering light now strikes you as a bit strange; you have never seen a sunrise or sunset like this before. Despite the different colors of the sunset, there is a red light shining everywhere. Everything in the room is now bathed in the red glow of the light pouring through the window, including the pictures of your deceased mom and dad on the bedroom dresser. Moving over to the bedroom dresser to get a closer look on the pictures gleaming in the red light, you see your reflection in the mirror. You are also washed with the same blood-like red glow from the sunrise. Yet on the outside there is no red glow to be seen, but everywhere remains dark.

You hear the loud blast of a trumpet, again. It is a loud, sustained, and piercing sound. You rush back over to the window, and you open it; the sound of the trumpet is so loud that it is almost deafening. The sound seems to be coming from the east, where the eastern sky is ablaze with the heavenly beauty of the spectacular sunrise.

You turn from the window to check the clock on the bedside table. It is ten minutes past midnight. A sunrise in the middle of the night; you smile at the idea. The time on the clock has stopped, possibly a power cut, you are thinking. You leave the bedroom to check the time on another clock; in the kitchen you check the battery-operated clock. However, the clock in the kitchen is giving the same time. As you are scratching your head, feeling puzzled, you hear another deafening blast of a trumpet. Again you go to the window to investigate. The clouds are still ablaze with the same radiant colors of shimmering light, looking like a glorious sunrise. But now there is something else that causes you to gasp with wonder. Instead of a rising sun, you see a dazzlingly bright light in the form of a man standing in the clouds, rising over the horizon.

The man in the clouds, shining with the brightness of the morning sun, is rapidly rising above the horizon. Gazing with wonder and amazement, you fall to your knees. Now you realize that this is not a sunrise. You are suddenly struck by the most fantastic thought: This could be the Son of God, rising like the sun in the eastern sky!

You stand at the window, viewing the dazzling form of his transcending light, while at the same time remembering the Bible prophesy about the Rapture– the catching away of born again believers just before the second coming of Jesus. Then the words of the scripture come to your mind:

"The face of Jesus shined like the sun on the Mount of Transfiguration." (Matthew 17:2)

And this thrilling thought almost blows your mind: The shining form that you now see could be the form of the transfigured Christ shining in his glorious splendor. The realization that this could be the Rapture– Christ returning for believers– fills you with an indescribable joy; you feel like a bubble that is about to burst wide open with irrepressible joy. You can hear your heart pounding with overwhelming jubilation– beating fast, as if you have been running in a race.

Grabbing your Bible from the table beside your bed, you frantically begin to turn the pages of the scriptures, searching for details about the Rapture to see if this stupendous shining phenomenon could possibly be the Rapture. You begin to hurriedly read about the prophecy of the Rapture, just before the second coming of Jesus:

"For the Lord Himself shall descend from heaven with a shout, with the voice of the archangel, and with the trump of God and the dead in Christ shall rise first. Then we who are alive and remain shall be caught up together with them in the clouds to meet the Lord in the air and so shall we ever be with the Lord. Wherefore comfort one another with these words." (1 Thessalonians 4:16)

You are now struck by the realization that you are suddenly experiencing the most sobering moment in your entire life- the most momentous moment of your existence: Your departure from this world- not by death, but by the First Resurrection, the resurrection to eternal life- a supernatural transformation, from mortality to immortality. You are now experiencing the real moment of truth.   The full impact of what is happening, and the awesome implications are now beginning to register. But your mind still cannot grasp the mind boggling magnitude of what is happening. You are shaken to the core with wonder and amazement.

You feel an irrepressible urge to shout praises to God.   Waving your hand ecstatically you run over to the window and looking on the shining form of the man in the clouds you shout, "Hallelujah! Hallelujah! Hallelujah! Glory! Glory to God in the Highest! You find yourself jumping up now like football fans when their team wins the super bowl. But unlike those fans, your joy will not be short lived, but it will last forever and ever. It's happening! It's really happening! The exodus of Christians from this world is about to begin. And you can't wait!

The sudden yearning you now feel to be with the Lord is beyond words. With awe and wonder, you stand before the window looking out at his glorious form shining with the brightness of the morning sun. The sky above is glowing with the brightness from the shining form in the clouds, but in spite of the light above, darkness still covers the earth below. Absolutely no light can be seen below from the glorious apparition that is shining with the intensity of the morning sun, except the blood red light that covers you as it shines through the window. You wonder about the meaning of such a strange phenomenon. And the urge you are now feeling to leave this earth is now increasing moment by moment as you view the surreal darkness covering the earth.

Suddenly you are struck by this horrendous thought: What if I'm not prepared! The teaching of the Bible about being prepared to go to heaven with Jesus now fills your mind with doubt and uncertainty. You wonder out loud, "Lord am I worthy?" And you fall to your knees, suddenly feeling the stab of guilt, shame and complete unworthiness.

So many questions are now whirling through your mind: Lord am I good enough? How do I know for certain that I've repented from all my sins? How can I know all my sins? It's hard enough to know every sin of commission, like committing sinful acts– doing what I shouldn't do. But how can I know about all my sins of omission, such as omitting to do righteous acts? I've not always done what you want me to do. How often I have failed to do the right thing, simply because

I've not loved others as myself? And how often the wrong kinds of thought cross my mind?

Again, you cry out to the Lord, "Dearest Lord, I'm not perfect, I'm so far from perfect! Lord, I've asked for forgiveness so many times before, but still, I sin. Oh Lord, have mercy on me a sinner."

Once more, you become conscious of the blood-red light coming from the man in the clouds, shining like the sun in the eastern sky. Your entire apartment is inundated with the blood-red light. And suddenly, you see yourself washed by the blood of Jesus. And now you have this wonderful epiphany: The red light from heaven is a sign that you have been washed by the blood of Jesus. Now everything is so clear. What can wash away your sins? Nothing but the blood of Jesus!

Standing there, covered by his blood, you begin to offer up a prayer of thanksgiving to God. You thank God for his saving grace. Indeed, you now see with a greater degree of clarity that you cannot be saved by your own righteousness. You can only be saved by the righteousness of Christ, who died for you to pay the penalty for all your sins. The words of this most enlightening scripture now comes to your mind, dispelling every shadow of doubt and uncertainty from you mind: "For by grace are you saved, through faith, and not of yourself. It is a gift. Not of works lest any man should boast." (Ephesians 2:8)

Unlike the teaching of every false religion, the Bible teaches that you cannot go to heaven through self-righteousness– through your good works. Why? Because no one can be good enough or holy enough to go to heaven. Moreover, self-righteousness always comes with the sin of pride, that you can be good enough for God. That is why Jesus declares," I am the way and the truth and the life. No one comes to the Father except through me" (John 14:6) Christianity is so different from false religions due to the belief that God and God alone gets the glory for your salvation! As you stand here covered by the blood-red light from heaven, you realize that the efficacious blood of Jesus is more than sufficient to cleanse you from all your sins. And you are on the way to your home in heaven, simply because of the precious cleansing blood of Christ, the Lord.

Called but Not Chosen

You decide to call Pastor Dyke to get his reaction about the incredible sight of the man coming in the clouds. You want to hear from the mouth of a great theologian like Pastor Dyke about what to do at a time like this. You feel confident that if anyone can explain this awesome midnight phenomenon, he certainly can. However, at this point, there is little doubt in your mind that the Rapture is about to take place. Your hands are shaking with uncontainable excitement as you are dialing the phone to reach the pastor. While you are waiting for him to answer the phone, the prophetic declaration of Jesus about his second coming echoes through the canyons of your mind: "You shall see the Son of man coming in the clouds." (Luke 21:27)

Answering the phone, he seems surprised to hear your voice. "Is everything all right? What's on your mind at this time of the night?" he asks, nonchalantly. The tone of his voice sounds alarmingly calm.

For a moment, you are speechless. Where has he been? Is he deaf and blind? The entire world must know. Stupefied and confused, you blurt out, "Look outside! Look to the eastern sky! Look!"

"Oh dear, you too? My son, Bryce, just woke up my wife and me to show us the sun rising in the middle of the night. Can you believe it? We looked, but didn't see anything. Maybe it was a UFO or some such thing. No reason to be alarmed. People see them all the time. They appear and then just vanish. By the way, I was going to call you to tell you about my new book. It's more exciting than any UFO sighting. The focus of the book is on the preaching of the prosperity gospel and how it can become the key to church growth. These days people don't want to hear about serving God, they only want to hear about God serving their needs.

We have to preach what the people want to hear. That's the secret to our phenomenal church growth, you know. Well, here I am rambling on. Be patient with me, my friend. Just hold on a couple minutes. Let me go to the east wing of the house and take another look outside. Who knows? Maybe now your UFO might be back."

While waiting for your pastor to take a look at the sky, you begin to think that something is terribly wrong. How could he not at least hear the trumpet sound? The sound was certainly loud enough to be heard by everyone. Then you hear his voice again on the phone saying, "I see nothing."

"Nothing?" You ask, conscious of the hollow sound in your voice; you are so deeply shocked.

"Nothing at all," he says again. "Perhaps what you saw is now gone."

You turn to look through the window of your bedroom. There in the eastern sky you can still see the man in the clouds, shining with the brightness of the morning sun, and surrounded with clouds ablaze with the colors of fiery red and flaming yellow, and with stunning shimmering shades of purple, and gloriously radiant with pink and amber. These words of the Scripture now echo in your mind, "They have ears to hear, but cannot hear, eyes to see, but cannot see."

You wonder how many religious leaders are just like your pastor– spiritually deaf and blind and yet functioning as spiritual leaders in the church, just like the carnal priest Eli in the Book of Samuel. Indeed, the pastor is your close friend, but over the years, you have become increasingly uncomfortable with his preaching and his lavish life style. His sermons, though always extremely eloquent, have increasingly become more entertaining and less spiritually enlightening or inspiring. He constantly avoids talking about the cross of Christ and the condemnation of sin. He tries hard not to offend the people, so he never preaches about unpleasant biblical subjects like hell, and God's wrath against sin. And as a result his church has grown by leaps and bounds. At times you have felt that he is more a politician than a servant of God– serving the will of the people rather than serving the will of God.

It is clear to you now that not all professed believers are witnessing this event. It is like the first coming of Christ; only the shepherds and the wise men could see the signs of his coming. Now at his return, only those who are ready to meet him with genuine faith will be able to see the sign of his coming. Ruefully, you realize that Pastor Dyke, like so many professed believers who have never possessed the Holy Spirit, will be left behind. This is the time when the tares will be separated from the wheat– false believers from true believers. So many professed Christians are called, but not chosen.

You remain speechless as you hold the phone to your ears– in total shock by your pastor's spiritual blindness. After a long pause, he repeats what he said before, "Perhaps what you saw is no longer there." ,

With your voice shaking with emotion you reply, "No, Pastor, Jesus is not gone. He's here, but you just can't see him. I'm sorry– so very sorry. Goodbye, Pastor."

There is another long, painful pause. "Goodbye," he finally says in a weak voice. Then he added, "I'm feeling so very sleepy all of a sudden," and hangs up the phone.

Suddenly a feeling of sadness washes over you. Tears of sorrow fill your eyes, not just for your pastor, who is also your friend, but for so many professed believers, who have never really had a relationship with Christ. This is the moment of truth for all Christians. Everyone that professes faith without possessing his Spirit will be left behind. The words of Jesus are being fulfilled right now: "Many are called, but few are chosen."

"Why me, Lord? Why choose me and not others?" you ask, while looking at the shining form in the cloud. And the answer wells up within you: it's all about grace, God's amazing grace. And this jolting thought enters your mind: "But for God's grace, there go I."

Rising from the Graves

You now feel compelled to join other believers who are seeing the same incredible phenomenon. You are convinced that all true believers are now seeing the man in the clouds, because there is absolutely no doubt in your mind that the form in the cloud is the Lord returning for believers. So you decide to drive over to your church to join other believers, who are possibly congregated there. As you hurriedly begin to get dressed, suddenly it occurs to you that soon you will be unclothed to be clothed with immortality. You remember the Bible prophecy: " You will be changed, in a moment in a twinkling of an eye." Soon you will have a new body, a celestial and an immortal body," Mortality will put on immortality." (I Corinthians 15:53)

Quickly getting dress, you begin to rush from your apartment to drive over to the church, when you pause to take another look at the glorious sight, looking so much like a spectacular sunrise on the horizon. Resplendent clouds surround the shining form of the man rising above the far horizon. Then you see another incredible phenomenon– not in the sky, but rising up to the sky.

As you continue to look through the eyes of your imagination, you now see numerous shining red lights looking like star lights caught up from the earth into the air, rising upward, taking a path toward the shining form in the eastern sky. The brightness of the form in the clouds is now increasing as it is rising higher and higher over the horizon. You watch with fascination, enthralled by the twinkling red lights moving upward higher and higher, heading straight up to the bright shining form of the Man in the clouds. But you are noticing now a most remarkable change in the color of the stars. As the stars pass from the dark shadows of the earth, the color of the stars change from blood red to pure white.

The words of the Bible describing the Rapture echo in your mind, giving you boundless joy: "For the Lord Himself shall descend from heaven with the voice of the archangel, and with the trumpet of God, and the dead in Christ shall rise first, then we who are alive shall be caught up to meet Him in the air, and so shall we ever be." (1Thessalonians 4:13)

You are convinced that the lights rising from the earth are believers who died in Christ and are now being resurrected, rising to meet Jesus in the air. The dead in Christ are now rising.

Steadfastly gazing on the shining form high above the earth, you see a change beginning to take place. A ring of gleaming white clouds is now being formed around the head of the shining form that you identify to be the Lord; he stands in the midst of the clouds that are ablaze with all the shimmering colors of a beautiful sunrise. And entering the ring of the gleaming white cloud, looking like a halo around the head of Christ, is the multitude of shining stars, which have been steadily ascending from the earth.

You can see many more stars ascending from the earth, streaming upward high into the air. A number of these star lights, can be seen ascending from a location near your home. And your heart suddenly leaps within you. You are watching shining red stars, twinkling in the darkness, rising from the location of the cemetery, where your parents are buried. Breathlessly you watch, as their colors are changed from blood red to pure white, when they escape the darkness of the earth below.

Now, you are feeling an overwhelming urge to see their graves. Grabbing your car keys from where it is hanging on the rack of keys in the kitchen, you bolt trough the front door of your apartment, rush down the flight of stairs leading to the main door of the apartment building, run across the parking lot, and quickly leap in your car. Then you speed away while thinking about this song: "There ain't no grave that can keep my body down."

While you are driving toward the cemetery, you are struck by the thought, "What if I'm caught up to heaven while driving this car? There could be an accident!" And then- in spite of all that is happening- you find yourself laughing out loud at such a ridiculous notion. What an idea! And you thought, "Of course, I can rest assured; the Lord in his divine wisdom is taking care of all the logistics of leaving this world." But you are rather surprised at yourself for feeling such levity- for finding humor at such a momentous time as this. Then you suddenly realize that the overwhelming ecstasy that you are now experiencing is no doubt the cause for your bizarre and surreal response. You feel so giddy with your new found freedom. And you just can't help yourself from blurting out, "Free at last! free at last!" The words of scripture now ring in your ear, "Whom the Son sets free is free indeed."

Taking the interstate highway to the cemetery, you are surprised that there is absolutely no traffic- not a single vehicle is seen on the highway. But what is even more surprising is the large number of cars parked on the side of the road, with every driver leaning back in their seat fast asleep. What is going on? You wonder! Getting off the highway at the next exit, you turn on to a road where construction workers have been busy working late at nights for some time. Driving by the construction site an unbelievable scene grabs your attention: The entire crew, numbering about ten construction workers, can be seen lying down on either side of the road, all sound asleep. Then recalling Pastor Dykes' comment about how sleepy he was feeling, provides the clue to the mystery of the sleepers: The physical slumber of unbelievers mirrors their spiritual slumber. All the world is now in deep slumber! Only believers are awake at this time, getting ready to take the final flight. For all true believers, the Rapture is the great awakening.

Passing through a residential area on your way to the cemetery, you suddenly glimpse a most precious and most joyful sight:- a house with a red light shining through its windows. Then within a distance of about two miles, you glimpse another, and then another until you are now up to about seven homes shining with the blood red light pouring down from heaven. Indeed, you are not alone: Other blood washed believers will be joining you on the flight of the Rapture.

As you see this wonderful sight- homes shining with the blood red light from heaven- the biblical account of the Passover comes to your mind: God promised the Israelites: When I see the blood, I will pass over you." Therefore, all the firstborn of the Israelites fleeing Egypt were spared from the angel of death that passed over their homes, because the blood of the lamb was plastered on the two door posts and door lintel of their homes. Certainly, God has made the same promise to all true believers whom he has chosen for heaven. God has said to you: When I see the blood of Jesus upon you, I will pass over your sins, forgiving all your sins, and take you to heaven to live eternally. Oh, the amazing grace of God!

While racing toward the cemetery, you see an innumerable multitude of lights shining like stars steadily ascending everywhere from the earth. They seem to be coming from numerous locations, extending beyond the circle of the horizon. You notice that the shining form of light and the ring of the shining white cloud, around his head, are steadily increasing in size as the steady stream of light ascending from the earth converge and merge into the ring of the shining white cloud. Indeed, it seems that the shining star lights are coming from everywhere, far beyond the horizon. You gaze with wonder at the awesome sight- an astounding pyramid of lights–from earth to heaven.

Overcome by the awesome sight, you realize that you are probably experiencing the same awe and wonder that the shepherds experienced when they witnessed the angelic host announcing and celebrating the first Christmas at the first coming of Christ. You are witnessing now the beginning or the first phase of Christ's second coming–the Rapture. And according to the Bible, his second coming to judge the world, and to eradicate evil from the world will be exceedingly more awesome than his first coming.

Within a few minutes, you are racing through the entrance of the cemetery. Parking your car near to the place where they are buried, you head straight to the graves of your mother and father. As you are running toward where they are buried, you look around the cemetery for any sign of the resurrection, but you see no sign in that area of the cemetery. Finally, you reach the grave site of your parents.

The sight before your eyes opens the floodgates of your eyes, releasing tears of joy. You see two gaping holes in the ground, as if someone had just uprooted two gigantic trees at the place where they were buried. Their graves are empty! They are gone! You fall down on your knees, feeling giddy with happiness; tears of joy are coursing down your face. With an overpowering emotion of rapturous bliss, you cry out, your voice sounding throughout the graveyard, "O Death where is thy sting? O Grave where is thy victory? Death and the Grave are swallowed up in victory today. Victory! Victory in Jesus my Savior forever!" Kneeling before the empty graves, you pour out your soul in worship to God. The thought that soon you will be seeing Jesus face to face as well as your parents fills you with indescribable ecstasy.

On the way back, moving more slowly through the graveyard, you again look around; this time you pause to look more carefully for any signs of believers rising from their graves. Happily, you see several empty graves. Each sight of an empty grave is so thrilling to see. But still you find the relatively small number of empty graves to be terribly disappointing and deeply disturbing.

The Sound of the Archangel

Driving from the cemetery, your attention is once again drawn to the awesome form of the man in the clouds. His hands are now outstretched, and he is shining with the brightness of the midday sun. You notice that the shining form of Jesus is still surrounded with the same clouds radiating the shimmering colors of a beautiful sunrise. The spectacular pyramid of lights, rising from the earth and ascending to Jesus, who is the Light of the World, is utterly breathtaking to behold. You wonder how many others are seeing what you are seeing. How are they responding to this wonder of wonders? Once again, you are feeling the need to join other believers who could be congregated at your church. You begin to wonder if living believers could be already caught up to meet Jesus in the air.

Suddenly, you realize that you are completely clueless as to exactly when, where and how believers will rise to meet Jesus in the air. You wonder if angels will be present now at the Rapture as they were present at Jesus's birth, at his resurrection and at his ascension.

Increasingly, you are feeling the need to be with other believers. You wonder if this urging is from the Spirit. You are now reminded that your faith is always strengthened by others: "Iron sharpens iron." You remember his promise, "Where two or three are gathered together in my name, there will I be in their midst to bless." Feeling convinced now that you need to be with other believers, you increase your speed to reach the church as quickly as possible.

Focusing on your driving and becoming preoccupied with thoughts about your parents' resurrection, you find yourself neglecting to look upon the heavenly phenomena as often as before. But now as you glance up to heaven, the sight you see brings your car to a screeching stop. You see an angel, transcendently radiant in appearance, descending from the sky.

Slowly, the angel descends, with unfurled wings glittering in the darkness. Below the descent of the angel, is a relatively small community park, where a few people are now congregated. The entire gathering of believers is covered in the glowing blood red light– the only light that is seen from the shining form in the clouds. With your heart pounding with excitement, and feeling the kind of ecstasy that you have never felt before, you jumped out the car, dart across the street, then run through the entrance of the park to join the believers who are all intently watching the descent of the angel.

While slowly descending the angel proclaims in a loud voice to the gathering, "Glory to God in the Highest! Behold he comes! Behold, Jesus, your Savior and Lord is coming in the clouds!"

The sound of his voice– like the brassy sound of a trumpet– reminds you of the trumpet sound you heard earlier. You now remember the Bible verse on the Rapture which says, "And the trump of God shall sound." You wonder: Could it be that the trumpet sound that you heard before was the voice of the archangel, who was actually the trump of God, waking up every believer at the mid night hour?

The shining angel, glowing with a radiant light, now stops his descent in midair a few feet above the ground and hovers with outstretched wings over the gathering of believers. The heavenly messenger glows with a dazzlingly white color, but his large wings are aglow with a shimmering light, the color of amber. You notice that the color of the angel's wings is the exact color of the amber cloud that now surrounds the feet of the Lord. The angel, looking down on the believers as he hovers above in midair, beckons for everyone to come closer together, his hands open wide in a welcoming gesture.

Looking around on the small gathering of believers, you are thrilled to see familiar faces. Ahead of you, standing close together, you see Lauren, Erin, Kyle and Paige– all members of your church. And also behind you other members– Moriah, Zachary and Kai. Suddenly you feel someone touching you on your right arm. Looking to the right, you see the smiling face of Bryce, Pastor Dyke's 12 year old son. Bryce is ecstatic and brimming with excitement. He seems so happy to see you. He clings close to you while you move forward with other believers to get as close as possible to the angel hovering above.

Everyone is now positioned directly beneath the angel. You and Bryce along with other believers wait silently and in deep reverence for the angel to speak. Every believer is still covered with the blood red light shining from the man in the clouds. Again, the thought enters your mind: We are washed by the blood of the Lamb. As you look up with boundless joy on the form shining like the sun, you wait with mounting excitement to hear from the heavenly messenger.

Looking down on the gathering consisting of about thirty people, the angel, without uttering a word, begins to make eye contact with each believer, as if quietly identifying each believer that is present. While he is looking down on each one, there is an adoring and a tender, loving expression on his face; the same kind of expression adults sometimes have when they see newborn babies. Finally, with a flourish of his hands and in his clarion voice the angel exults,

"Saints of the most high God, sons and daughters of Almighty God, to you who are called the redeemed, the bride of Christ, the light of the world, and the salt of the earth, to you who have been chosen by God to be born again of the Spirit to become new creatures in Christ, I bring you good news. I bring you good tidings of great joy. For unto you have returned this day the Savior, who is Christ, the Lord."

He pauses for a moment, then, pointing to the shining figure in the clouds high above, he cries out triumphantly, the sound of his thunderous voice reverberating in the heart of every believer,

"Behold, he comes in the cloud!" The angel then points to the stars still ascending from the earth to the form in the clouds shining now like the sun, "See how the dead in Christ are rising from their graves. Shining like stars, they ascend to meet the Lord in the air. Only these, who have been justified by faith in Christ, their Savior, can take part in the first resurrection, the resurrection of the just. The dead in Christ throughout all the ages and from every nation are now rising to receive their eternal reward, the gift of eternal life. And now you who are alive, you, who put your trust in Christ Jesus as Savior and Lord, soon you shall also be rising to meet the Lord in the air."

The angel pauses again, looking down on the upturned faces of the believers. You, like everyone standing beneath the angel, are completely mesmerized by the awesome message of God delivered by such an awesome messenger. While the angel was speaking, his face was framed with the zeal and the passion of an evangelist; but now as he begins to cast his eyes on the upturned face of each believer, again the same tender, adoring, loving expression returns to his face.

Slowly and gradually folding his wings, he begins to descend to the ground. His descent produces an immediate rippling effect on the group of believers clustered underneath him. The believers directly underneath step back a few feet from the area directly underneath the angel, causing everyone standing behind them to also step back leaving a ring of space in the center of the gathering for the angel to enter. Slowly, he descends until his feet touches the ground.

Coming down to your eye level and standing in the midst of the gathering, the angel turns to look on the congregation of believers encircling him. There is a look of wonder in his eyes as he moves through the crowd to get closer to each believer. It seems that he is just as awed by the believers as they are awed by him. He looks directly at you for a moment with the expression of someone desiring to hug an adorable baby. It looks like he is about to hug you but then, still smiling tenderly he turns to Bryce and says in a soft, gentle tone, "Bryce, you have many questions, I know. Soon you will understand everything."

Stunned that the angel knew Bryce by name, you blurt out, "Oh, you know his name!"

"I know the name of everyone here," he says, his face beaming with good humor. "We are sent from heaven to watch over you. We are your guardians. You could say that we're the babysitters for all God's children."

Moving back to the center of the small gathering the angel again addresses the believers. Everyone is still covered with the blood red light from above. "I know everyone is asking this question: Why so many others who profess to follow Christ are not here? I will remind you of the answer that the Lord has given you. Our Lord says,' On the day of judgment, many shall say, we have preached in your name and cast out devils in your name and have done many things in your name. But I shall say, I know you not, depart from me, you workers of iniquity.' They are not here with you because it is not enough for believers to merely profess to know Christ. They must also possess his Spirit in their heart; they must truly love God like every one of you here has loved him."

It seems that everyone is beginning now to be more at ease; every believer is visibly more relaxed. Apparently, it is becoming increasingly obvious to them now that they are not in the company of an alien from heaven but a heavenly caretaker and friend. You marvel to see how the same reverence, the same warm tender smile and look of adoration on the angel's face, are also on the faces of everyone in the gathering. It is as if what you are feeling is being mirrored by the angel and everyone else. Indeed, for the first time in your life, you are experiencing what it is like to be one in the spirit, and what it is like to be truly in one accord spiritually.

Caught Up

The angel looking upward points up to the sky. Now, no more ascending star lights from the earth can be seen. The lights are all gone from the earth, all have merged in the shining white halo around the head of Jesus, who is still surrounded by the clouds. And the clouds are still gleaming with the shimmering colors of the most glorious sunrise.

The angel says, "It is time. The first resurrection has been completed. The rising of the living children of God is next. Behold the Lord! He waits to meet you in the air. And I will see you there."

He pauses to look around one last time on every one with the same tender, adoring, and loving expression on his face. Then smiling sweetly, he extends his shining wings of amber upward, and in a flash of light, he is gone. The angel instantly disappears high above, into the shining cloud of amber encircling the feet of Jesus as he stands in the midst of the clouds.

"I'll see you up there!" Bryce calls out after the angel.

Now you ask Bryce the question that has been on your mind from the time you first saw him here alone without his parents: "What happen to your dad, Pastor Dyke, and also your mom?"

Bryce sighs ruefully, "When I woke them up to show them what I saw and heard, they couldn't see the Lord in the clouds, and couldn't hear the trumpet. So when they went back to sleep, I decided to walk over to the church where I found a bunch of people standing outside the church. And they were all looking up at Jesus just like me. Then when we saw the angel flying down from the sky toward this park, everyone decided to come over here and they brought me along. I'm really happy to be with Jesus. I love Jesus! It would be great if Mom and Dad could be here, though. Do you think they'll be angry with me for leaving?"

You hug Bryce, knowing that soon he will not have a single care in the world. Indeed, he will be free from all cares. But now he is worried about his parents so you say "I don't think they'll be angry with you for leaving, but I think they'll be angry with themselves for not leaving with you. When you get to heaven ask Jesus why your parents couldn't see him like you. I have a lot of questions for Jesus too."

Bryce eyes widened, with curiosity. "What kind of questions?" he asks.

"Like, for example, how will the world explain our departure? Will they say that we were taken away by aliens from space? Will they say that believers in Christ were in league with extra-terrestrial beings? How will the world change after we are gone? Will there be hell on earth when the power of darkness rules this world? But, I think the Lord will, no doubt, answer all our questions before we can even ask them."

You take his hand into yours. Then, turning to the gathering, you call out, "Let's all join our hands together, and as we wait to go to our Lord, let's sing this song for the last time, "Just as I am, without one plea, O Lamb of God, I come, I come."

Everyone complied, joyously joining their hands together– everyone covered with the blood red light shining from the man in the clouds. They all sing with you the well- known hymn that has led so many to Christ. Every face in the gathering of believers is turned upward, looking steadfastly on the form of Jesus in the clouds as they sing. The sound of the singing fills the entire park, sounding sweeter than the singing of any song that you have ever heard. As you sing, you begin to see a new and a deeper meaning in the words of the song. While you are singing, you can hear the words of this Scripture echoing through the canyons of your mind:

"Behold I show you a mystery: We shall not all sleep, but we shall be changed in a moment, in a twinkling of an eye, at the last trump; for the trumpet shall sound, and the dead shall be raised incorruptible, and we shall be changed." (1 Corinthians 15:51-52)

While you are singing, you look steadfastly upon the shining form of Jesus surrounded by shining clouds. Now, everything around you is becoming strangely dimmed as you watch the glorious sight above.

A sudden, incredible change is coming over you. You are experiencing a wondrous exponential expansion of every sensory perception throughout your entire body. Your sense of sight, hearing, touch, smell, and taste are infinitely magnified. You are now seeing what your eyes have never seen before and hearing what your ears have never heard before; in all of your sensory perception there is the sweetest sensation– an incredible vividness, and a new dimension of awareness. It is like the experience of one who was always blind but now can see or one who was always deaf but now can hear the sweetest sound of music.

And in a moment, in a twinkling of an eye, your body has changed, transfigured to a body of light. Wonder of wonders! Your body has been transformed from a natural body to a spiritual body. Looking around, you see that everyone has undergone the same kind of change, becoming bodies of pure light. Everyone is so gloriously fascinated with their new bodies that they abruptly release the hand that they are holding to feel and to examine their glorified and immortal bodies.

Then you begin to rise! Higher and higher, you rise! With the sudden change from mortality to immortality, you can now see and understand with perfect clarity the meaning of everything around you. In a moment of time, all of life's mysteries are now clearly understood. Just a moment ago, you were seeing reality through a glass darkly, but now you are face to face with reality, as you cross over the threshold from time to eternity. And you know that you know that you know– the moment when faith becomes sight is the moment when immortality begins, and the moment when perfect love is experienced for the first time. Oh perfect love, at last to be truly one with God!

You can see clearly now! What appeared to be clouds ablaze with the colors of a beautiful sunrise- resplendent with colors of fiery red and flaming yellow, and with stunning shimmering shades of purple and radiant with pink and amber– were really a host of angels, an innumerable number of them surrounding Jesus. The enormous size of Jesus towers high above the earth reaching far into the heavens. The shining, bright cloud at his feet is revealed as a stupendous host of angels, having wings with the colors of amber, pink, purple and blue. And the shining cloud of angels surrounding his waist and chest have wings with colors of fiery red and flaming yellow. How exceedingly joyful it is to see that the white cloud in the shape of a halo around his head are the resurrected saints of God, believers in Christ, all clothed in shining garments of pure white. And in the midst of the angels and believers, you see Jesus laughing joyously, his eyes focused on you.

The Lord is still shining with the brilliance of the sun, but his features are now clearly visible. You see his outstretched hands and the nail prints in his hands; you remember his great sacrifice of love for you. He opens wide his arms to welcome you. He is looking at you now with loving tenderness and with eyes of compassion. As you are rising to meet Jesus in the air, you see your resurrected mother and father calling out to you. You also see many dear friends waving to you. But now you only want to see Jesus, face to face. There is no one like Jesus; no one loves you like Jesus.

You have come to know him as the Lily of the Valley, the Bright and Morning Star, and the Fairest of Ten Thousand to your soul. But he is so infinitely more to you that no words can describe the love you are now feeling for the Lord. He is not only your Lord and Savior, but your dearest and closest friend.

Like a child waking up from a bad dream, you rush into his comforting arms, and through tears of joy, a cry of love and adoration comes from the depths of your soul. You cry out, "My Lord and my God!" And with joy unspeakable and full of the glory of God, you join in the triumphant cry of all the saints: "Home at last, home at last, thank God Almighty, we are home at last!" The kind of joy and happiness that you are now feeling is truly beyond words. The glorious joy that you and every believer are sharing now with Jesus, while surrounded by the host of angels, no one has ever known nor will ever know nor can ever imagine. Indeed, it is truly the kind of joy that is so unspeakable and so full of God's glory. And so shall we be with the Lord forever and ever and evermore.

Lessons Learned in Odyssey

Many Christians who profess faith in Christ will not be going to heaven. It is not enough just to profess faith as a Christian, you must also possess the Spirit of God. Only born again Christians possess the Spirit. When his Spirit is in you, the love of God will flow from you. Jesus says "if you love me, you will keep my commandment." (John 14:15) He also says, "By this shall all men know you are my disciples, by how much you love one another." (John 13:35) According to the Bible, believers without the works or manifestations of love are not truly born again; they are not born of the Spirit. Therefore such believers will not be caught up in the Rapture.

Believers at the time of the rapture will be resurrected with glorified bodies like the glorified body of Jesus when he was resurrected from the dead. They will have a supernatural body. The Bible declares, "So also is the resurrection of the dead. It is sown in corruption, it is raised in incorruption. It is sown in dishonor, it is raised in glory; it is sown in weakness, it is raised in power. It is sown a natural body, it is raised a spiritual body." (I Corinthians 15:42-44) The new and transformed bodies of believers will no longer be under the curse of sin. There will be no more sorrow. The Bible says that God will wipe away all tears. All believers with glorified bodies will be immortal like Jesus, living forever in heaven.

Reflections

Tick, tock, tick, tock! Time marches on. The older we get, the faster time seems to go. Like grains of sand moving through an hour glass, so the days of our lives seem to run out with every beat of our heart and every breath that we take. Time marches on not only with the rhythm of our beating hearts and the rhythm of our breathing, but also with the rhythm of the sun rising, the sun setting, seasons changing, generations changing and people aging—everything and everyone marred and disfigured by the ravages of marching time.

From birth to death– tick, tock – time marches on. To the young time is a friend, but to the old an enemy. Young people look forward to the future with anticipation, while the old look backward to the past with regret. The young wish they could travel faster forward through time to experience the promise of the future, but the old, remembering the carefree days of youth, wish they could go backward in time. One imagines and envisions the future; the other remembers and dreams of the past.

During the formative years, time takes the young from weakness to strength. With youthful giddiness and excitement about life, they soar on the wings of time to the zenith of their development. But soon– ah, far too soon– the declining years begin and the young grows old, and the days grow dark. Therefore, the Bible says, "Remember thy creator in the days of your youth, before the evil days come."

To the old, the evil days come with the ravages of time, when hopes fade and dreams dissolve in the murky shadows of the past. Sadly, and so despairingly for the old, time does not take them from weakness to strength like the young. But with the declining years of the old, they go from strength to weakness. The old grows weaker with the heavy burden of too many years; aging brings a growing awareness of one's mortality. Consequently the elderly do not view favorably the marching of time,

Sooner or later, with growing alarm, we all shall see the warning signs of the times; and we shall shudder inwardly with fear. In quiet desperation we must live our lives, trampled and worn away by the march of unrelenting time. As we approach the end of life, we experience this rude awakening: Dead end ahead! Then comes the shocking realization: Life is too short! Too soon our journey of life comes to an end. Finally, when the march of time is forever halted with the last heartbeat and the last breath, time stops for us. Death comes; temporal existence ends for all with the last heartbeat, the last breath and with the last "tick" of time. The inexorable flowing river of time carries all from the cradle to the grave. But thank God, for all Christians, who believe in the resurrection power of Christ, the grave is not the end. We shall experience a new beginning! From the grave to a world unknown, to a new dimension of existence– the spiritual dimension. Surrounded by the endless ocean of eternity, we shall live again.

Comparing Time to Eternity

I have described time as flowing, moving, and marching– a sequence of events constantly changing, like the ticking of a clock: tick, tock, tick tock. However, the description of eternity is quite different. The Bible reveals that unlike our temporal existence that is constantly changing with passing events, our eternal existence in heaven will be changeless– peaceful and restful. Perhaps the unchanging stillness and the sublime peace that can be experienced, while viewing the countless shining stars suspended in the universe reaching into infinity, provides a sense of what eternity might be like. At such times the myriad points of light shining in the darkness of infinite space seem changeless, motionless, restful, and profoundly peaceful. Transcending in its sublimity, eternity, like infinity, is a reflection of the divine attributes of our eternal and infinite God.

While time– the medium for the passage of events in our temporal world– has a beginning and an end, eternity has no beginning and no ending. Eternity can be compared to a circle, without a beginning and without an ending. However, time is revealed to be linear: a straight line, having a beginning and an ending– a sequence of events. Indeed, time is made up of the past, present, and the future, but eternity consists only of the endless present, with the past and the future becoming part of the eternal present. If the view of eternity seems inconceivable and mind boggling to us, it is simply because we are temporal beings, existing in the dimension of time. Although we will become eternal beings like God, possessing life without end, yet as creatures of time, we can never become truly timeless like God, because we have a beginning in time, but God, who created time, has no beginning.

Revisiting Time in Eternity

As eternal beings that were once creatures of time, our memories of the past will undoubtedly play a key role in the worship of God throughout eternity. Indeed, the memory of God's mercy and great love will be the cause for our eternal gratitude to God. Because of the memory that God so loved us that he sacrificed his Son for our sins, we shall forever in heaven express our love and thanksgiving through worship.

In light of the fact that we are creatures of time, and have experienced the ravages of time, we will be able to praise God in a way the angels can never praise him. For example, the angels could never praise God for his great mercy and grace, because they never experienced his salvation from the terrible curse of sin. Only believers, who were once sinners, can ever know that where sin abounded, grace did much more abound. Indeed, we will appreciate Jesus, the Light of the World and the Savior from sin, far more than the angels, because we- unlike angels- will always remember the dreadful darkness of the world, when we were once children of darkness, and completely lost in sin.

One can only wonder what it will be like in heaven when the stream of time enters the ocean of eternity to become a part of eternity. Will we be able to travel through time to re-enter the ages past to witness the crucifixion and the resurrection of the Lamb of God again, as an act of worship, just as we now repeatedly remember his death and resurrection? Revisiting the past as heavenly time travelers would be a sacred act of worship for the redeemed in heaven, as it is an act of worship now to remember the death of Christ, who gave his life for our sins. Of course, this kind of thinking about heaven must necessarily be viewed as somewhat speculative, since our knowledge about heaven is so limited. But we wait for the time to come, when there will be an end to all speculations: The Bible says that in heaven we will have perfect knowledge, and "we shall know even as we are known."

In the final analysis, we now can only "look though a glass darkly" on our eternal future. Indeed, as it was pointed out before, our knowledge of the future is limited to only what God has revealed through his word. In his great wisdom God has revealed to us as creatures of time, only certain things about our eternal future. Therefore, we can only imagine or speculate about what the future in heaven will be like, based on glimpses of heaven from biblical revelations. However, according to the Bible, the wonders of heaven will far exceed anything we can ever imagine. The Bible says, "Eyes have not seen, nor ears have heard all the wonderful things that God has in store for us." The wonders of heaven's transcending beauty are so inconceivable to creatures of time that it is far beyond our wildest imagination. As we look forward to the incredibly glorious future that awaits us, we can only say, as the Christians living during the time of the early church used to say, "Maranatha!" Come now, O Lord! Indeed, the transcending beauty of heaven will only be exceeded by the transcending beauty of the glorified Son of God. But now here in the shadow land of this world, we can only imagine.

www.ingramcontent.com/pod-product-compliance
Lightning Source LLC
Chambersburg PA
CBHW070015100426
42740CB00013B/2506